WITH OPEN HEART

W9-DBH-937

MICHEL QUOIST

With Open Heart

Translated by Colette Copeland

CROSSROAD • NEW YORK

1986

The Crossroad Publishing Company
370 Lexington Avenue, New York, N.Y. 10017

Originally published in France by
Les Éditions Ouvrières, Paris
under the Title *A Coeur Ouvert*
© Les Éditions Ouvrières 1981

Translation © Gill and Macmillan Ltd 1983

All rights reserved. No part of this book may be reproduced,
stored in a retrieval system, or transmitted, in any form
or by any means, electronic, mechanical, photocopying,
recording or otherwise, without the written permission of
The Crossroad Publishing Company.

Printed in the United States of America

Library of Congress Cataloging in Publication Data

Quoist, Michel.
With open heart.

Translation of: A coeur ouvert.
1. Meditations. 2. Quoist, Michel. I. Title.
BX2183.Q56713 1983   248.4   83-7607
ISBN 0-8245-0614-6   0-8245-0569-7 (pbk.)

Introduction

To My Readers and Friends

I've always gathered up left-over pieces of bread from dinner tables. Perhaps it's because when I was a child I would be fascinated by the sight of my grandmother sweeping crumbs off the white tablecloth after a big holiday meal. The crumbs were destined for the birds – nothing was wasted. Later, when I was older, the starving eyes of emaciated children stared at me hauntingly from posters and magazines. Perhaps, too, that is a reason. Those eyes seemed to implore me silently for a few of those pieces of bread. Still later, I actually saw those children – live, before my very eyes – fight with pigs for their swill. I can no longer throw food away, not even crumbs.

I have neither the time nor the means, my friends, to offer you a beautiful book. I can offer you only a few pieces, not to say crumbs of life. But perhaps with enough crumbs one can be nourished.

I've been collecting my crumbs and turning them into words and sentences for a long time. I've written in small notebooks, on bits of paper, on the back of envelopes. I've written just before bedtime, jotting down a few fragments of my day. I've often written while travelling, because that's when I've felt really free – on planes, trains, in waiting rooms. I've written during conferences and tediously long meetings. I've written everywhere, and at any time of the day or night.

I write for *myself*. For me, as for many others, it is a way of meditating and praying. Short or long, these pauses allow me to see beyond the boundaries of my own life, beyond man's life, beyond the world's life. Now and then I catch sight of Jesus Christ and I hear his calls in the distance, all too frequently drowned by my own noises. My reactions are, like yours perhaps, weak, sometimes non-existent. That's how it is. I just wanted to tell you. I don't want you to think that I'm different from you.

It is fashionable to interview well-known personalities and have them tell their life story and express their thoughts. And from their words, books are made. Some have wanted me to 'talk'. I have refused. I have difficulty expressing myself before one person. I have none before an audience of five hundred or a thousand. Their attention and expressions open me up.

Some friends have read a few of my 'crumbs'. They've told me that I shouldn't throw them away, that I should offer them as nourishment to those who want them. This I accepted, preferring to offer my own notes rather than answer an interviewer's questions. I thought it would seem more authentic.

Since you intend reading this book I'd like to explain a few things about how I put it together so that you will better understand me and not be too surprised about certain points.

This book isn't a diary. Although biographical in parts, it has more to do with my personal thoughts and reactions over the years; but they aren't set down chronologically. I used to have many notes and several copybooks. I lost two copious notebooks and — especially at the start of my ministry — I threw away lots of notes. What's more, I never wrote regularly. So don't be surprised at the gaps; don't think that I give importance to certain aspects of life and neglect others. I repeat, these pages do not reflect all my past and present life, or all my thoughts. If there are long periods of silence it is because I either didn't write anything or I threw away what I had written.

You won't find unity of style in this book because the conditions in which I write are varied and many. There are descriptions, thoughts, prayers, shouts. . . . There are moments where I become so frustrated with the inadequacy of words to express the life bursting in me that it comes out in images and rough poems. For me these poems are prayers.

I offer you my *own* thoughts. Obviously I do not intend to

2

foist them on you. When writing, I write to myself, I address myself. You are free to put yourself in my place, but I would be upset if you thought for one moment that I was trying to 'convert' you to 'my' ideas. On the other hand, I would be happy if I could offer you the opportunity to reflect upon your own life, if I caused you to search for the path of Christ and help bring forth your own prayer. To arrive at this, you must read this book slowly, a few pages at a time, perhaps even only a few paragraphs at a time. And then . . . put the book away. My mother used to say to me: 'Don't eat so fast! Chew your food slowly, you'll get more out of it.' And it's true, even if the food consists of only a few crumbs.

With one exception, I didn't want to dig up buried memories. Not because they've faded — they haven't — but because I was afraid of embellishing them as one tends to do with memories. There is nothing in this book, not even a few hastily scribbled lines, that wasn't written on the moment. Of course I had to write and rewrite, but the essentials were already there, spontaneously put down on paper. I have respected this spontaneity even if, in reading over my notes, I was tempted to colour a judgment here or a thought there.

Having hesitated and asked for advice, I decided against assembling my notes by subject and following some sort of chronological order. At times I have put certain passages together simply to make their reading easier.

Many of my friends in the priesthood could have written passages similar to the ones I am offering you. Obviously everyone's story is different — events and encounters aren't the same ones, points of view are divergent and even at times opposed — but the strong step towards humanity and towards Christ, the efforts to serve them both, are identical. I am above all conscious of the fact that there are lives richer, more real, more devoted, than mine. They remain hidden. I'm almost ashamed to speak while others are silent. They are the ones who should be speaking. For my part, alas, I haven't often chosen or wanted to stand at the front of the stage. I have, on the contrary, often resisted and fled to the wings. But to some of my friends I have said: 'If you can speak and be heard, speak! If you can write and be read, write! You must.' The same was said to me and I repeated it in turn to myself. And I have been given so much by so many that I hope, despite all, that my crumbs in turn can fortify you. The Lord uses all to nourish the hungry.

Friends, readers, Christ awaits us. I want you to meet him and only him because I am sure that my hunger, like yours, whatever its external manifestations, is a hunger for Jesus Christ.

Michel Quoist

My Land, My Roots

To help the reader understand what I'm trying to do in this book, I am told I should provide something more than the brief biographical blurb on the back of my books.

One doesn't know much about your background, a friend remarked recently. You ought to write about it to clarify certain events, reflections and dialogues which you talk about in your book.

He's right, of course. To understand the fruit or flowers of a tree, you have to know about the earth and the roots.

Here they are.

My origins

I was born in Le Havre on 18 June 1921 to Le Havre-born parents. I have an unmarried sister who has been involved in my work as my secretary, more or less since the beginning of my ministry. I owe much to her, much more than the typing of manuscripts. My father was a chartered accountant, my mother a housewife. I come from the middle class – which some theoreticians deny exists because they don't belong to it. The middle classes will tell you from experience, however, that it feels like being of mixed blood. There was a time I thought being middle class was to be tainted. But I quickly discovered that, spiritual options aside, being at the crossroads of two worlds – on condition that I let myself be myself, open and receptive – allowed me to understand both those worlds. Difficult, but not impossible. Perhaps, then, it's because of my middle-class background that I have been able to work both in the working and middle-class worlds (not, as many believe, exclusively in the working-class one).

Perhaps, too, that is why my books have found their way to such a diverse audience: kings of friendly nations, dockers, and Indians of the Andes alike.

Searching for a meaning to my life

I was raised in a very Christian way by my mother who was a regular churchgoer. My father was not a believer, and there too I was divided, inheriting something of his questions and doubts, even if they weren't clearly expressed. I've often said that, in my case, received education, rather than education through experience, had evidently been a case of water off a duck's back.

When I discovered the *living* Jesus Christ it was in the street and through J., a militant member of the JOC (Catholic working-class youth movement). Having brutally lost my father at the age of twelve and a half, I had been working since the age of fourteen. I worked as a messenger for an insurance company, then for a forwarding agent dealing in cotton. It was while running from office to office that I met J. He became my friend, opened my eyes to others and involved me in little jobs for the JOC — the first one being a job selling calendars — and, little by little, by putting me on the path to my brothers, he put me on the path to Jesus Christ.

Very early on I had started, on my own, looking for a meaning to my life and life in general. I just couldn't believe that this enormous mass of humanity into which I had not asked to be born, this impressive, wonderful yet terrible universe where people fought, bled, died . . . I just couldn't believe it was as demented as it seemed. Personally I refused to be a river without a source, a path that led nowhere. I often thought that if I didn't find any — to my mind, valid — reasons for living, I could certainly find ample ones for not living. Because I haven't forgotten my own questioning youth, I've always taken young people and their questions seriously. They are not to be taken lightly, shrugged off with an indulgent smile. There is real anguish behind some of those questions. Before teaching young people how to live, they must be taught *why* they live.

I arrived at the idea of a God by myself. It turned out to be the 'God of philosophers and scholars'. But I wanted

6

more. I wanted a God who was interested in me, a God I could meet, with whom I could talk; very briefly, a God who would respect and . . . love me.

At the same time I observed the people around me. The mystery of the human being dazzled me. Through him I sought a path, a way. There must be, I thought, a vital lead, a 'something' to be found in everyone which perhaps led to the source. At first I thought it was life itself, for life flows in everyone; it comes from afar, is transmitted from one person to another, developed and fiercely defended to the death. But I discovered that there was something even more important than life, something that life was given up for — and that was love. Yes, *Love*. Deep in every human heart, without exception, the overriding emotion was love. I undertook to verify this in others and in myself. I imagined myself rejected, deprived of hugs and kisses, handshakes, words and looks; alone, horribly alone. I couldn't bear it. I imagined myself incapable of loving, locked into my prison of loneliness where all doors were firmly shut with no hope of escape. I would skip night-classes and walk the streets instead. Then I would return home at the usual time so as not to arouse any suspicions. I would stroll around, almost always alone, looking at apartment buildings, wondering about the families and couples, young and old, behind the lighted windows or closed shutters, all of whom, successfully or not were trying to love in their own way. I listened to the pop songs of the day: they sang of nothing but love. I would skim through pornographic magazines which the fellows at work would ask me, a kid, to buy for them, and discover in them the body's 'hunger'. And despite the heavy subject matter, it seemed to me that it was those fellows' way of crying out for love. I concluded that man, that strange animal with the power of reason, lived only for and because of love. It was his *reason for living*. I was now ready for the REVELATION.

Meeting the living Christ

One evening, returning from a JOC meeting with my friend J., I asked him: 'Who is Jesus Christ for you?' J., in his own way, told me about his faith in the *living* Jesus Christ. And together, and later with others, we embarked on a search for

Jesus Christ in the Scriptures and in life. For me it was a stunning experience. Certain words in the New Testament (I had no knowledge of the Old Testament until I entered the seminary) are still a source for quenching my thirsts. I recall how I would rush to that source for a long drink. It's no accident that after ten years and more I can still remember the places where J. and I read, re-read and savoured certain passages in the Scripture — on the beach after a swim, on a bicycle trip along a certain river, in such and such a street one night in the light of a street lamp. A naïve sort of reading, some will say. Perhaps, but I do know that it changed my life. Even today, I believe that these words were 'living words', and the only regret I have is that I wasn't as faithful to them as I could have been.

I grew up nourished by the Gospel. And out of this daily nourishment, I am sure, come my present reservations, and my restrained anger, at those sorcerer's apprentices who seem to reduce the Scriptures to some sort of 'object' of study. Listening to them, or reading them, I suffer just as if a person near and dear to me were being dissected alive, before me, just to explain, without risk of error, the depth and meaning of my love.

Thus God had become 'someone' for me. He was LOVE and Jesus Christ was Love incarnate. Man was the fruit of Love and completely created by this Love. Together, as a team, in my case a team of JOC militants, we were building the great Body of Christ. My life, in its minutest details, and the life of the world, had a meaning and was worth living. But it had to be told to one and all that LIFE WAS JESUS CHRIST. With all my strength, I joined my friends in singing: 'We will renew our brothers' christianity.'

Learning from life

At work I learned how slow the passage of time can be, especially during long interminable afternoons (2 p.m. to 7 p.m., five hours without a break!). Unhappily for me, I had been rapidly promoted to a pen-pushing job where I was chained to a desk pretending to be busy. Not wanting to attract any adverse attention from my boss, I didn't dare wander away from my desk too often. So there I was, reduced to dropping pencils and erasers on the floor just to give myself a pretext for getting up and taking a little walk around my desk.

I also learned how easily jealousy and hatred can begin. In summer, when the sun shone outside the office windows, I would dream of the sea where my friends, who were still in school, splashed about in the water. Why them and not me, or anyone else for that matter? I couldn't wait for the eight days paid holiday which the company (in advance of other companies it must be said) generously bestowed upon its faithful employees! The strikes of 1936 and the *Front populaire* later got us fifteen days paid leave and reduced work hours. This was all I needed to convince me of the necessity and effectiveness of the workers' struggle.

I had discovered the essentials – not in books but by thinking about life, alone, in the dark, and later by the light of the Gospel. My path was mapped out, my habits formed and I would not deviate from them. I think I can say that what I discovered about God, mankind and the world had always been there in life. And that's partly where I found answers to questions which had been haunting me. I firmly believe that the risen Christ is present in the heart of the world but we don't see him because we're blind. He talks, but we don't hear him because we're deaf.

Later, I turned to books and became an avid reader. Only then did I really 'study'. Sometimes I nearly got carried away by my books but I can confidently say that all they did was to confirm, in more detail, what I had already discovered. They revealed nothing of major importance that I didn't already know. Hence my skepticism regarding certain forms of study which are cut off from the daily realities of life. Often the *mind* is formed but the *person* isn't. Some think that studying and learning are enough to form a whole person and equate thinking well with living well.

A JOC member . . . and dying

I rose in the ranks of the JOC very quickly, at first locally, then 'federally' (there were, at the time, two JOC 'federations' in the diocese of Rouen; one in the 'capital', the other in Le Havre, with the latter covering the area which is today the diocese of Le Havre).

All my evenings and Saturday afternoons were taken up with the JOC. I was happy.

In 1937 I attended the Tenth JOC Anniversary Conference in Paris for three memorable days during which 85,000 members thronged in the streets of the capital, the underground and the Parc des Princes. Being then one of the leaders, I gave myself to it all wholeheartedly, and by the end of the three days, I was dead tired. On the train home, I picked at a spot on my nose. It got infected and the following morning at work, I became ill. By the afternoon, I was being rushed to hospital and two days later I was dying, the doctors having given up the fight to save my life. 'There's nothing more to be done, leave him in peace . . .' they said. Everyone was resigned to my impending death — my mother, my friend J., the hospital's head nun who promised there and then that she would send me to Lourdes if I recovered. I recovered. The doctors were baffled.

I had known I was going to die; I'd overheard my aunt say as much. Silently I had offered up my life for my friends, the JOC and the world. It was all very simple. I had read about young JOC members dying while giving their all. I think I was proud to be among them. What surprised me was that I was surrounded by anguish and sorrow (I had lost my sight but I could hear and guess everything that was happening around me). What surprised me too was that I wasn't offered the last rites. I didn't dare ask for them myself. Otherwise, I waited for death, imagining my own funeral with wry amusement while I waited and waited. I don't know how others see me, but for my part I know that in my life and its big(!) moments I've never been able to take myself too seriously, even though I've always tried to live all my moments, big or small, seriously.

A priest? Why not!

The following year I joined the diocesan pilgrimage to Lourdes as a stretcher-bearer. On the train back I met a priest with whom I had a long discussion about the *Action Catholique*. From then on I was to see him often. I admired and respected him, but still I dared — you had to be bold, such was his personality — to disagree with him on the subject of vocation.

We argued about it every time we met.

One night, after visiting, in my capacity as JOC federal official, a JOC 'division' which needed help, I dropped in to see him despite the late hour. The old argument flared up again. Suddenly, as if impressed by my ardour, the priest said to me: 'Why don't you become a priest?' Why? Why? Because I didn't have a vocation, that's why! He then told me in a few words that a vocation wasn't some kind of mysterious calling, but . . . well, I don't even remember the rest. I think I stopped listening. He concluded very quickly: 'It's just a thought . . . I won't bring it up again.' (Later he confided in me that it had been in fact 'just a thought', without premeditation.)

We smoked a last cigarette and I took my leave.

Cycling across town on my rickety old bicycle, I kept thinking: 'Well, why not? Why not?' and once I got home, I got on my knees and said to the Lord: 'If you want it, then I want it.' For my part, the decision was made. Not once since that moment have I doubted my vocation, which doesn't mean that it was all easy.

One can meet God in the street.

A few months later I was in a seminary for 'late vocations'. I had to spend the next three years catching up on missed study. I was to receive an 'education' which would match, *on every level*, the one I'd learned in life. I was ready for everything, for Jesus Christ and for this humanity for which I so desperately wanted to do so much. But I had to be patient, very patient; I had to let myself be shaped, honed, totally transformed. It's difficult these days to imagine what a shock such a total and sudden change of life and direction can be for an 18-year-old boy, never mind older ones like some of my friends.

Soon after I entered the seminary I began receiving a lot of mail. Many of my friends were shattered by my decision and wanted to keep in close touch with me. I felt the same. However, one of the directors called me to his office and told me I should discourage all this correspondence. He said I'd have to 'cut myself off from the world' because — I still remember his very words — 'one can only meet God in the

11

silence and the desert' and that 'Jesus himself, before speaking out, had lived hidden for 30 years'. Wrong, I thought, that's *wrong*. I was so sure of it. I had found God in the streets, in action, and if it took silence and desert to bring God to people, then 99 per cent of humanity would not only *not* love him, they'd never *meet* him!

I was appalled. But I reacted quickly. I kept repeating to myself: 'It's wrong, it's wrong!' I'm sure that's when I caught this burning desire to tell people that Jesus resurrected was waiting for them *in the heart of the world* to build with them the Kingdom of the Father. I didn't know how I was going to explain this to them at the time, but I didn't let that worry me. I had faith. I knew, though, that if I was alert and receptive, some day the Lord would show me how.

Having come to this decision, I continued at the seminary, scrupulously doing all that was required of me.

Praying before every face

The war interrupted my studies. The seminary shut down and I was sent to a large Catholic school to act as a supervisor. I was to continue my Latin studies with the chaplain there. I was instructed not to get too friendly with the students. During recess and study periods, or in the dormitory, before 120 boys (some were my age), I was not to read or talk but simply keep an eye on them and take note of anyone who broke the rules. Well, every experience is useful. I learned to control a group in the most difficult way – just by a look. I learned to scrutinise faces; I learned that without a word or gesture, one could meet and get to know a person, and that this person, wonder of wonders, was unique. I prayed before every face. Mysterious ties were being forged. When the evacuations separated us, some of them cried. As for me, I just forced my face into a smile.

The war and German labour camps

I returned to the seminary. There were only a few of us and life was quite different. Classes were so small that they felt more like private tuition sessions.

The following year – my final one – the seminarians grew

in number. Much was changing. I had gained an unexpected measure of confidence from my superiors, who put me in charge of my fellow seminarians. A few of us organised working teams and holiday camps. We rebuilt destroyed churches and communities, discovering as we went along a 'dechristianised' countryside.

I went to a seminary in Rouen for higher studies. It was, at the start, a standard, 'classical' place; later it became more 'open'. Some of my fellow seminarians really suffered there but after what I had gone through, everything seemed easy. They were my age but I often found them to be terribly young. Not that it was surprising – our respective lives so far had been so different.

Some of us lived as a team. We dreamed of a communal life some time in the future. But our attempts weren't always successful. Like everything else in life, it was easy in the imagination, difficult in practice.

It was wartime. Some of my friends were prisoners, others were in the Resistance, and yet others were being shipped off to the STO (*Service Travail Obligatoire* – Labour Camps) in Germany. There was a divergence of positions taken and choices made. I had decided to wait until I was called up by the STO; I wanted to be with the hundreds and thousands of young people labouring and suffering in Germany. I received a travel warrant and presented myself to the authorities. That day there were so many people to process that many were sent home and asked to wait until further notice. I was running a children's holiday camp when my 'further notice' arrived. The children badly need the fresh air, food and peace of the country and if I left now they would be deprived of the rest of their holiday. I did some quick thinking – in the time the authorities would take looking for me, I could stay with the children and make sure they had their full holiday. I tore up my travel warrant. For the sake of those kids, I offered up any and all consequences of my action to God and calmly waited for the police to arrive. Well, I'm still waiting for them! They never came – and to whom or what I owed this I'll never know. In my life I have seen the blossoming of so many flowers and fruit I haven't planted that I've thought I owed them to many unknown, secret hearts offering me their strength and vigour. The following story is proof.

A few months before getting my sub-diaconate, that moment of final decision, with no warning whatsoever, I woke up one morning more or less blind. I asked one of my colleagues to guide me discreetly to the chapel for prayers and communion, then to take me to the superior's office. I was immediately despatched to a specialist who examined me carefully. 'What on earth have you done to your eyes! I've never seen anything like it. You're bloody well done for now! You might as well kiss the priesthood goodbye!' Luckily I had been warned that he was a bit 'coarse' and that swearing and insulting his patients was a way of hiding his feelings, but also . . . that he was an excellent diagnostician! And that was that. I was decked out in jet-black spectacles with strict orders never to remove them and given a prescription for some medicine which, I was told, would 'do absolutely nothing' for me.

Back at the seminary, everyone was shocked. I decided to see the year out. I listened to lectures; friends would take turns to read notes back to me. I was already discovering a new way of learning. I admired the sensitivity of some of my friends who surrounded me with quiet support. I was touched by their many gestures of help and friendship, even if I couldn't always recognise them.

Everyone prayed for my recovery — except me. However deeply I was hit, I was still surprised at the fierce way some wanted to extract a 'miracle' from God. I didn't ask for miracles. Right from the first day, the first hours, of my blindness I had said to myself: I'm sure that the Lord wants me to dedicate my life to his service and that of my brothers. If he decides it won't be in the role of a priest, so be it. It'll be in some other role. Questions, tears, these were only a waste of time and energy and I had none to waste. There was nothing heroic about the way I felt — only a calm certainty that you can't go wrong if you're receptive. Heroism is being totally loyal, all your life, in every small detail. I am no hero.

So, once more, I was surrounded by people who wouldn't give up. I was sent to the Quinze-Vingts Hospital in Paris to consult the top specialists, then on to Geneva. All the diagnoses confirmed the first one: I was, and would remain, near-blind.

When I returned from Switzerland, I went to see my

irascible doctor. He took off my spectacles and I said: 'I can see!' 'Idiot!' he countered, and examined my eyes. 'You're lying — hardly the thing for a priest to do, is it?' he added. But I insisted I could see. 'Impossible,' he said. Then he put me through a couple of tests and the evidence couldn't be denied. I really could see! He didn't take credit for my recovery. He simply swore a bit more than usual.

A priest — finally!

I was ordained in July 1947. I celebrated my first mass in Rouen Prison before a large number of prisoners, two of whom had been sentenced to death. They were to be executed shortly after and they had specifically asked that I prepare them for it. My first mass was their last. One of the condemned men had, I think, strangled a rival with his bare hands. I remember noticing that even a murderer was capable of real love. He spoke very little of himself actually, but a lot of the woman he had lived with and whom he would be leaving destitute. 'Pray for her,' he kept saying. 'Pray for her.'

This was yet another encounter which confirmed my unfailing faith in the human being. In each one, whatever his origins, culture, behaviour, a little ember glows: life, generated by the breath of the love of the Father. No, I hadn't been mistaken — man was born of love and for love.

After all these years of preparation, I was finally a priest and I could now re-join the world outside. Having been won over by Jesus Christ, I was not immune to the temptation of joining a religious community and leading a life of pure contemplation. My superiors, on the other hand, saw me as part of the *Missions de France* (French missions). I decided to stay in the diocese with my friends. That's where I would serve the Church.

Study from books, but mostly from life

I waited impatiently for my letter of appointment. I wasn't interested in taking a vacation first. I just wanted to get to work. The cardinal (Cardinal Petit de Julleville, my arch-bishop) told me that, on the recommendation of my professors, he was sending me, along with two of my colleagues to the *Institut Catholique* in Paris for further studies. Was I going to spend my life studying, then, while the world waited for Jesus Christ to be revealed to it? But, naturally, I obeyed.

In Paris, we took the courses set by the Social and Political Sciences Institute but all three of us, having been thrown together in this way, took advantage of the situation and exchanged thoughts and opinions, prayed together and invented 'spiritual exercises'. It was thought that our courses would prepare us to put into practice in the outside world what we had learned in five years of religious community living. Here we came into contact with founders and directors of missions: the Paris Mission, Community Parishes, Missions on Wheels . . . Father Godin's book, *France, Country of Missions*, had just been published, giving rise to a sharp awareness of the 'de-christianisation' of the masses. For me, this was a fruitful period. I learned that one could live as a priest without having a ministry.

I learned from my courses but, with due respect to my professors, I learned even more from my own sociological research, which I undertook on the request of my arch-bishop, into a large working-class section of Rouen. It was fascinating! I was still studying people but not as individuals this time — rather, in groups and by scientific methods. I discovered that a neighbourhood was a large living body of people encompassing smaller groupings and centres where the little man and the influential man came together, where development and progress were precise and limited. But I also discovered — and I have the figures to prove it — that mortality among the young was higher, that delinquency flourished here more than elsewhere, that religion was practised in inverse proportion to the density of slums in the census taken of the area, and so on. While proceeding scientifically, I also tried to pursue things spiritually. As a priest I considered it my duty to take on and 'offer up' this neighbourhood while studying it, and the more I studied it, the more responsible I felt. I prayed daily while meeting people, and at night I prayed over this life revealed to me through maps and statistics. I had devised a method of research, inventing my own terminology and ways of comparison. In particular, I devised a way of using tracing paper

16

to draw on, then superimposing the different sheets so as to analyse precisely the correlations between the various pressures acting on people. It seems that this was an innovation and I was given credit for the idea, even in far-off places such as the United States. I doubt, though, if I was in fact the first person to come up with this idea. Anyway, that's all it took to make me noticed and labelled a 'specialist'. The National Scientific Research Institute and the Ministry of Reconstruction and Town Planning showed interest in my work. Father Lebret, the founder and director of the *Economie et Humanisme* publishing house, came to Rouen to see what I was doing. And from that visit grew a solid, respectful friendship, as well as our future collaboration. I was to work with him on a work entitled *L'Equipe d'enquête et d'action* (published by *Economie et Humanisme*, now out of print), and later with other researchers on *L'Enquête urbaine* (an analysis of towns and neighbourhoods, published by *Presses Universitaires*). I was also appointed to the National Commission of Religious Sociology.

A stillborn 'sociologist'

I was finally notified that I would be getting a full-time appointment. I had waited ten years for this moment, yet, this time, I asked my archbishop to allow me to finish my research first. I had begun writing it up and was to present it as my doctoral thesis a few months later. But he refused, saying that he needed me. Rouen needed a vicar in its main parish, which I had studied well in the course of my research and knew inside out. So I expected to be assigned to it. As it turned out, however, I was appointed to Le Havre's Saint-Marie parish, an important working-class district.

I finished writing my thesis in the evenings and in my spare time when I had any (it was published as a book entitled *Man and the City*, by *Editions Ouvrières-Economie et Humanisme*, and is now out of print). I was able to go to Paris to defend my thesis only because – and this was a condition met by my superior – I was able to find someone to replace me in my daily cathechism classes while I was gone.

Shortly after, the Assembly of Cardinals and Archbishops of France requested on two occasions that I be released to go and co-ordinate and direct urban socio-religious projects all over France (Father Boulard had done a similar and wonderful job in rural areas). On both occasions my archbishop turned down the Assembly's request. Not long after, it was the turn of Father Lebret who requested, on behalf of *Economie et Humanisme*, that I be sent to Brazil for a year. There I would direct a team of sociologists commissioned by the government to study the city of São Paolo. The request was denied. As usual, I bowed to the decision, but this time I couldn't help feeling a bit upset. I was young, impatient to discover the world and work in it. It was only natural that I would get upset at all these refusals. A year's work in Brazil, unlike the work in Rouen, was so well backed and organised that I had been very enthusiastic about the project. Among other things, we would have had access to a small aeroplane and aerial photography. An aeroplane! What luxury, what possibilities! Psychologists can rejoice: tied as I was to a chair and a desk, I dreamed of flying!

At the end of my chat with my archbishop in which he had refused to let me go to Brazil, I smiled and said: 'Too bad. I'd have loved to go. But, you'll see, one day I *will* go to Brazil.' A few years later I was in São Paolo and I repaired immediately to the *Economie et Humanisme* offices and asked to see the survey the sociologists had carried out. I was taken to a large room in which a great mass of voluminous paperwork was neatly filed. I asked what purpose all this work had served. 'None,' I was told. It seemed that once the work had been completed it was no longer useful; the city was so huge and had grown so rapidly in the meantime that the survey was out of date before it was even completed. Inwardly, I could only laugh. I didn't waste any time on futile regrets — I certainly didn't regret having obeyed my superiors.

I participated in a few more sociological conferences, lectured in France and abroad, as always in my own time. For a couple of years I studied the work of the National Commission of Religious Sociology. But as my diocese didn't appoint me to any work in the field of sociology, I gradually drifted away from it. Thus my sociological career came to an end. Many couldn't understand why and regretted it. Some tell me they still regret it. I hadn't chosen to undertake any studies beyond the seminary – quite the contrary; I hadn't chosen to go beyond a doctoral thesis, had never taken myself for the 'specialist' which others saw me as, or had any such ambitions. Still I was surprised at the lack of logic displayed by my superiors even though I ignored those who urged me to protest. I had been made a curate, so I decided to dedicate myself to being just that – fourth curate of the parish of Sainte-Marie du Havre.

When life becomes a prayer: the book of prayers

I won't go into my parochial activities, not because they weren't important (they were – I learned much and lived through much), but because I don't want to add to this already long narrative. All I want is to show how, in spite of – indeed, perhaps because of – the mistakes of my superiors, the Lord allowed me to serve him and my brethren in a completely different, totally unexpected way.

From my very first day in the parish of Sainte-Marie I began receiving many young people and adults, single or married. Many came to see me, perhaps because they felt they could relax with me and talk about their lives. I listened to them for hours; I wanted to know everything about their existence, their joys and sorrows. I wasn't content merely to give them bits of advice or lecture them about going to church more often.

I vigorously welcomed my new duties and tried to nourish my prayers with them. I even began praying aloud in front of my visitors at the end of their visits. I would ask the resurrected Christ, who I was certain was present in their lives, to reveal himself in those lives and make his intentions and desires known. This sort of thing was unusual at the time, but I noticed that it gave unexpected depth to these visits. My friends, for their part, largely benefited I think. They always returned, and so did others.

One night, after my visitors had left – I no longer recall who they were – I wrote down the words we had together addressed to the Lord. To these words I added: 'This is the prayer we made up together. Repeat it to yourselves and if you want, continue to pray this way always. It is in this gesture that Christ waits for you; this is where you must join him and work with him.' I slipped copies of it into envelopes and sent them off to that evening's visitors. From that day on, I was to repeat this ritual often. When I had time, I would rewrite the prayer in more polished form, trying to make a poem out of it. This is how some of my friends learned to pray regularly.

One day, towards the end of my 'sociological' (!) career, I presented a paper in Belgium. I was waiting in the office of the priest who had invited me over, and thumbing through some magazines on an end table. A package of photocopied material was beside them. Glancing through them I discovered one of my 'prayers'. This was the first of many discoveries of my prayers; I was astounded to find them, copied and passed from person to person — a rapid distribution with no effort at all on my part. I was impressed to say the least, and after conferring with some of my friends, I decided to collect these prayers, work on them a bit and add on some personal thoughts. I then submitted the lot in manuscript to the *Editions Ouvrières/Economie et Humanisme* publishers who, in spite of the novelty of the manuscript, decided to publish. The book turned out to be a totally unexpected success. Edition succeeded edition without interruption — they are still being put out today after all of thirty years! More than two million copies of *Prayers of Life* (published as *Prayers* in the U.S.A.) have been sold world-wide, and translated into twenty-four languages. Prodigious!

I hasten to add here that none of this success is of my doing. All I did was to listen to and observe life, and to try and meet the resurrected Christ. Out of that grew my efforts to express, in simple language, man's dialogue with his Lord. It wasn't a case of one fine day deciding to write a book of prayers. Each of these prayers was 'lived' and experienced before being written down. I was just an instrument, a collector, the one who put it together. Only life can engender life. We should thank those who have offered up their lives in communion; one day they will know that they have nourished multitudes. I know it for a fact, through the numerous testimonials and letters which I have received, and continue to receive, from all over the world.*

And so I found myself on a new path. Once more it was a path I had not chosen myself.

*I had at the start destroyed these letters as I received them. I regret doing that now. But I was young and afraid I could be tempted to take credit for the success of the book, and keep some of the thank-you letters from readers to myself.

My other books followed without much planning on my part; in fact, at times none at all. Every chapter of *The Christian Response* (published as *The Meaning of Success* in the U.S.A.) for example, is a condensation of a collection requested by one group of people or another. Gradually, from life itself and people's needs, whether felt or expressed, these chapters came into being. I had noticed that my audience took in not the text as a whole but an image here, a sentence there which condensed and expressed an essential idea, and struck the right chord. So I would photocopy them and hand them out. And again these sheets of paper were circulated. Some appeared in magazines. In the end, I put them all together into a book. So far, a million and a half copies have been printed, it's been translated into twenty-three languages and is distributed all over the world.

The teenage publications (published by *Éditions Ouvrières*), *Aimer, ou le journal de Dany (Loving, or Danny's diary)*, *Donner, ou le journal d'Anne-Marie (The Journal of Anne-Marie)* are actually real diaries. All the characters exist in real life; the stories are true, but they are of course properly edited into books. At the time, these books attempted to answer adolescents' questions. I had systematically and scientifically collected these questions from many schools, colleges and polytechnics.

Both diaries were published for the young people of France, but to my great surprise, they were picked up and translated into eleven languages. I came across them in all the countries I visited. Adolescents everywhere identified with Danny and Anne-Marie, like the little barefoot Indian girl I met in the pampas of north-eastern Argentina who stared at me silently — then, overcome at seeing her book's author standing before her, blurted out: 'Anne-Marie is me!' Mystery of mankind, of youth, so alike, with the same problems, the same evolution, whatever their race, their milieu and the degree of their country's development. I would add too, that whatever the year those diaries appeared in, they are still relevant today, with today's young readers making whatever adaptations are necessary.

I won't go into my other books, but I do want to mention *Visages du Christ* which I published later with *Éditions*

Ouvrières. I had noticed that many people were interested in biographical details, and I had myself been profoundly moved by reading short works dealing with the lives of JOC members who had died young. So I wanted to give my readers accounts — not of saints but of Christians, outstanding but not inaccessible, people readers could identify with. I was certain that many had written letters and detailed diaries which had to be located and published. They would show today's 'faces of Jesus Christ'. Sixteen books were the result of this idea and their distribution is very large. I don't regret not being able to spend more time researching and polishing these texts. The world's need of such writings is too urgent to wait.

This is how my 'ministry of books' came into being and was developed. More than 6 million copies of my books (not counting the *Visages du Christ* collection) are in existence. Would I have written them had I stayed on the course of religious sociology? I can only say that I'm forever thankful to the Lord for not letting me waste time in futile regrets and even more futile battles.

Pastoral Ministry and Ministry of the Word

I remained a curate for barely four years. My archbishop asked me to take on the directorship of all the urban youth movements in Le Havre and its region (the present diocese of Le Havre). And so I moved out to the *Centrale d'Action Catholique* — a centre for Catholic movements where I stayed for seventeen years, at first as federal chaplain of seven *Action Catholique* movements, including the JOC and JOCF. I managed in time to have other priests join us to help with the work. It was hard work, a heavy burden, but it was also exciting and fulfilling. I lived with young people who brought me so much — they are still my most appreciated of teachers.

As soon as my first book came out, invitations to lectures, retreats, week-end visits and seminars came pouring in, both locally and from abroad. Rather than ebb, they grew in number and I found a new activity opening up before me, one which would be demanding of my time. There was no question of taking time off from my parish. I would make do with whatever extra time I could muster, and organise my time as best I could. My archbishop had given me permission to accept these invitations within reason, and I accepted what I could because I didn't want to pass up any chance of 'broadcasting the Lord's name'. To tell the truth, I never understood why I should be invited over anyone else. In terms of competence, my fellow priests could have done as well. But their names were unknown, that's all. People tend to think that authors of books are better speakers somehow. What's more, the further away a speaker comes from, the more he's appreciated and listened to! Fame comes very easily away from home. For a long time I've felt all this to be a sort of injustice towards my fellow priests. Today I tell myself that perhaps I haven't made enough use of this fame attached to my name which seems to attract so many audiences. In any case, I try to be responsible. I would have frightened myself had I myself looked for this notoriety. I have mobilised the attention of thousands (in lectures, books on radio and television) so many times that I would consider myself guilty of an abuse of confidence if my spoken or written words weren't genuine and didn't sow the right seeds. Happily, as I've said before, there are others who nourish these seeds into living plants.

So, because of my books, I started to travel. I point this out in order to clarify observations on foreign countries which I make throughout this book. I think I can say that I've never been a tourist, not even a 'spiritual' tourist. With one or two exceptions, my travels have been the result of invitations from bishops and various committees, with the trips organised in advance. (I'm often asked what languages I speak — only French, I'm afraid. All the countries I visit provide me with interpreters.)

Action Catholique and other Movements

My main job was, as it always is, the one my archbishop appointed me to in the diocese. I went from one meeting to another, from one movement to another, from one social milieu to another, and from one age group to another. This diversity can only be described as beneficial — it prevented me from becoming a 'party man', in the pejorative sense of the word, that is, sectarian and narrow. I was forced to see all sides to a problem, to discover all the different places in which the Lord is to be found, to respect the opinions and differences of individuals and groups. I did all I could to serve well the movements to which I was chaplain, but I never wanted to be their slave. I truly believe that, born out of the Church, they were and still are *providential ways for the Church to evangelise*; but I have never held that any of the elements characterising the movements, whatever their merits or otherwise, had the force of dogma. On the other hand, I don't think I had a very strong group sense or mentality, probably because of my previous work in research where I was essentially on my own, and the general progression of my thought as well as my ever present fascination with the mystery of the individual.

All in all, I don't think we'll ever realise or appreciate the vastness of the *Action Catholique*'s contribution to the Church both in France and elsewhere.

The sometimes dangerous gulf between spiritual and worldly commitment will, unhappily, open up now and then; how much better it would be if the gulf didn't exist at all, and if those who doubt could see that both commitments should be fused into one movement of love, in and through Jesus Christ, for the Kingdom of the Father.

In Latin America

I first met Abbé Pierre when we invited him to come to Le Havre. We had formed a welcoming committee to meet him, and followed that up with action against poverty. This all took place in a year of dreadful freakish cold weather, out of which developed what the Abbé termed 'the insurrection of charity'. We put together a film, a long piece of footage on poverty in the city, which many people found hard to forgive me for. I was accused of having faked the film — that's how difficult it was for the better-off to believe that such poverty could actually exist. Projected onto a giant screen at the *Gare Maritime* before an audience of 5,000, it served as an introduction to Abbé Pierre's frightening indictment. Many achievements were to grow out of that event. Many a conscience was jolted, and 'conversions' even took place. For myself, I admired the man profoundly and what I gained from him was an unfailing lasting friendship.

Some time later, Abbé Pierre invited me to accompany him on one of his tours of the Emmaus Communities which are spread all over the world. This trip was to cover South America, and I found the invitation tempting. I asked my bishop if he could spare me for a little over a month; I would take this time off in lieu of holidays since I never took them anyway (summers were usually spent organising youth camps, so personal holidays were not possible). He agreed, not knowing that he was thus introducing me to new apostolic directions. For the very first time I helped myself to my income from royalties which, so far, I had used only to defray secretarial and car expenses; otherwise I had never used this money on myself – to this day, it is given away either through institutions or directly, as the need arises. I've always lived like an ordinary priest. This time, however, I had to pay for the trip. Before leaving I went to see Monsignor Riobé whom I had known at the *Institut Catholique*. At the request of the French Episcopate, which had responded to John XXIII's call, he had started sending volunteer priests to South America. He asked me to observe and think about this project and to let him have my impressions – which I did.

I won't talk about the visit itself – just the consequences. When I returned to France, I reported back to Father Riobé. He read my report, then told me that in his position he had no time at all to spare for the South American aid project, and would I join him and do the work in his place. I told him that was impossible but he insisted, saying he would ask my bishop. From experience I could have told him that my bishop would reject the whole idea. And a rejection is what he got. He persisted however, taking every opportunity to deftly argue his case. On his fifth or sixth request, Cardinal Martin, my archbishop, finally gave in, *on condition I did not neglect any part of my diocesan duties*. All this activity took place without me – I had no say in anything. So I found myself, on top of everything else, secretary general of the French episcopal committee for South America (CEFAL).

None of us, not myself, Cardinal Martin or Father Riobé, had foreseen the development of CEFAL. To the few priests already sent to South America, others were gradually added.

Seven years later when I left the secretariat, the number had risen to 185.

Every month or so I worked with Father Riobé for a few hours. The rest of the time I was on my own. He trusted me fully to get on with the job.

I spent hours meeting with priests and their bishops; organising sessions and sorting them out; appointing volunteers, helping them settle in, visiting them and bringing them together. All told it was like running a real diocese, relatively small in priests but geographically huge. A whole continent in fact! The problems were mostly related to the enormous distances and, in contrast, made our problems in France look very trifling indeed. I shall never forget it!

Geographically, I worked on the European side of things, in particular with our friends in Belgium, Spain, Holland and Italy. In Church matters, I worked on a world-wide scale. Meetings of the General Council of the pontifical commission for South America took me regularly to the Vatican. I knew nothing of the Roman Curia and had never wished to approach it. However, I must say that I did meet some admirable and serious men there, faithful to the service of the Church; but I also observed that bureaucrats in the Vatican are much the same as bureaucrats anywhere else. No matter how qualified and admirable and saintly they may be, they are still very far removed from the man in the street. Only very exceptional people can understand problems solely through files and paperwork. Bits of paper will never replace knowledge gained from reality and daily life. During the committee meetings I was haunted by thoughts of my fellow priests and all those who were suffering and struggling over there in South America: what would they think, what would they say if they saw us now, discussing and deciding their work for them. There we were presenting detailed texts, blow-by-blow accounts and final reports which would probably *never* be read.

What we need is men at the top who are also down-to-earth people and who can from time to time return to basics. In spite of everything, I don't regret those encounters – they were an enriching experience – and there were many more to come through my South American ministry. I spent some time in Rome, a few times during the Synods. The bishops were assembled there and I was able to see all those connected with South America, and organise, with Father Riobé, meetings by country, inquiring about their needs so as to be able to more effectively carry out our modest aid programme. First with Monsignor Lebourgeois, then on my own, I represented the Church of France at Medellin.* It was a great moment in the history of the Church of South America. That's where the decision to combat poverty was firmly taken. Despite all the manoeuvres, the oppositions, the persecutions, we got past the turning point and would not essentially be challenged again.

And so I worked for seven years establishing and developing the secretariat-general of CEFAL. I tried to turn it into the best possible instrument of mutual aid between the French and South American Churches and, in particular, the French volunteer priests to South America. I feel, too, that in doing all this I didn't neglect my normal diocesan duties. To be honest, I don't know how I managed to do both; I was so convinced I could never handle two jobs at once. I figured I had reached my limits before, but this proved how wrong I was and that time is more elastic than we think.

The South American Exchange Association

On my return from my first trip to South America with Abbé Pierre, even before being named secretary general of the episcopal committee. I had decided to personally contribute something to the apostolic efforts of the South Americans. One thing was clear: even if the Churches with large numbers of priests heeded the pope's call and sent some of their priests to South America, their aid, in relation to the enormous needs of that continent, could never amount to more than a drop in the ocean. What was needed was to help the South Americans to establish what I called 'a pastorate without priests' (I meant, of course, with very few priests). Over there I had asked the people in charge many times: 'Since you've got valuable lay people — *Action Catholique* militants and catechists — why don't you assign them, either

*The South American bishops, with the blessing of Rome, have created a body known as CELAM (in French). This body regularly organises a general assembly of delegates elected from all the bishoprics. A report is put together, voted on, then submitted to the pope for his approval. It is then recognised as a guide for all the continent's pastorate. Paul VI opened Medellin in Columbia; John Paul opened Puebla in Mexico.

27

on a part-time or full-time basis, to evangelistic duties?' The response was the same everywhere: 'We would have to pay them a salary and we haven't got the money.' I decided to raise that money in France, so I founded the 'South American exchange' association. Monsignor Riobé accepted its presidency, and was later replaced by Monsigner Bardonne, Bishop of Châlons-sur-Marne.

The premise of the association is simple. Christian people commit themselves to making a *regular* donation one or more times a month (it works out at 10 French francs a time, about £1 or $2) for one to three years. When we get requests from South America asking us if we could help to send so-and-so somewhere to do a certain job, we honour the request on the basis of regular donations. The member-donors receive a regular news-sheet on the activities of the lay people they are funding in South America. It's a small gesture — since its inception, the association has been paying a monthly salary to some eighty odd full-time people — but it has the merit, quite apart from the wonderful achievements of these people, of ensuring their presence on the spot. It isn't too difficult to find money for buildings, but it is hard to find regular money to keep people working on the spot. The reports we get from South America confirm that we're on the right track. Only recently, a very thoughtful letter from Dom Helder Camara said as much.

And it's all thanks to a small team of dedicated, discreet and faithful (a rarity) lay people. (They can be reached at: Secretariat, Exchange American Latine, 20 rue Saint-Martin, 76600 Le Havre, France.)

Return to Basics

In my diocese I have always sought to be what I really am — an ordinary priest. It's a bit difficult though when you've been doing things out of the ordinary, and especially when people (mostly outsiders) insist on making a big fuss over you. I used to talk as little as possible of my extra-diocesan activities. My colleagues were very nice but I didn't want to make them feel left out, or be thought 'different' from them. I don't know if it worked. I hope so. I would truly be upset if I thought I had unwittingly put anyone out.

These days, however, I wonder sometimes if I wasn't too silent. Perhaps I missed the point, perhaps I should have shared more with my brothers.

In any case, I didn't trust myself. I wanted to be sure I was acting out of genuine faith and not for the sake of celebrity. Could I be as serious and committed in the limelight, before big audiences, as I was in the shadows, before six or seven people?

The priests I preached to at retreats would tell me: 'It's different for you. You're not like us, leading a life of baptisms, marriages, burials — sometimes, sadly, too many burials. You don't really understand. You can't.' And I would think, on the one hand, that I wouldn't be able to carry on working with young people much longer; and on the other hand, that I had got so much out of my South American work that it was only fair that others, just as qualified as me, should have their chance at it. In short, I wanted to return to ordinary parish life, with a little time set aside for writing and attending conferences, seminars and retreats — invitations which still kept coming. I had asked to be named curate, and so I was. I returned to Sainte-Marie du Havre where I had been seventeen years earlier.

I would be less than honest, however, if I said that I never felt restricted in this parish, even when a little later the bishop gave us the responsibility of a second parish. Compared to South America, the parish seemed tiny, and my duties as easy as pie! But that didn't really bother me. I was convinced that everything has its merit and importance, and that the nature of our work wasn't as important as the dedication we brought to it. I would think of that on weekday evenings while celebrating mass before seven or eight old ladies. There too, in that little chapel, I could reach the whole world if I had a mind to. I tried.

I wasn't to remain at Sainte-Marie for long. Six years later, quite unexpectedly, I was again assigned elsewhere.

Today

At present, in my part-time diocesan work, I am in charge of vocations. I am also responsible for the co-ordination of the bishopric in independent centres and, once more, I am chaplain to the *Action Catholique* movements. In my extra-diocesan time, I try to keep on writing and accepting what I can of the invitations to retreats, reunions, conferences in France and abroad.

And there you have it, my friends and readers. If you've been patient enough to read me this far, I offer you these few words. Do be indulgent — it's taken a lot out of me to write them, especially on the subject of my personal thoughts and development, and the work that I was asked to do. I find it difficult to talk about myself. But my friend was right: the following pages will be easier for you to understand now that you know something of their background. You may even come to the same conclusion, which I've often repeated: it is not a waste of time to let ourselves be guided and to try and do what has been asked of us the best way we can. Like everyone else — let me say it again — I can but *try*. The only thing I regret is not having always succeeded, because I do believe that through all the events in our lives, Jesus Christ resurrected invites us, and waits.

If only we could be faithful.

1

For the dead branch which will never again bear new leaves or flowers or fruit, the branch that life has forsaken, one wonderful final option still remains: to be added to a fire and produce light and warmth for those around it.

Lord, tonight I offer you the dead branches of my day. In the fire of your love they will be transformed.

But on stormy evenings, alas, I often leave my dead branches on the ground to rot.

2

I have nothing to give to another; but I have the duty to open him to his own life, to allow him to be himself — infinitely richer and more beautiful than he could ever be if I tried to enrich and shape him only from the outside. All is *within* him because the source lies in his heart of hearts. But so many obstacles prevent it from surfacing! I must be the one to help it spring forth and smash the concrete around him, and in him. I must be the one to help him dig and search, and dig some more, to find the source. And from that source, life will spring.

3

I saw this inscription in a youth centre: 'Happy are those who can laugh at themselves — they haven't finished laughing.' What a wonderful sentiment. I laugh at myself more often these days. I feel like laughing. I want to make others laugh. People take themselves too seriously. How foolish!

I don't think I take myself seriously. Other people, especially those abroad, stick serious labels like 'celebrity' on me. Strange . . . I think they're probably projecting their vision of me. They no longer see me for what I am — a man, or a priest like any other.

4

No writing that doesn't contain at least a modicum of life flowing through the words and sentences can nourish a reader. Only life can give life.

5

Everything begins with 'Let us create man in our image.' God loves mankind. The passion of mankind resides in God. He loved man to the point of Passion, that is, solidarity pushed to the limits: death.

Following in the footsteps of Jesus Christ, one cannot be Christian without this passion, this solidarity with others — all others — and without living this passion to the point of suffering and death.

You have to pick your side, it's said.

I pick the side of mankind . . . but I'm still a long way from living up to the demands of my choice!

6

It's not a matter of straining out towards God, but relaxing before him.

7

Tomorrow God isn't going to ask
   What did you dream?
   What did you think?
   What did you plan?
   What did you preach?
He's going to ask *What did you do?*

8

Only the deeply rooted can bear fruit. Now, modern man is dissatisfied and forever searching for his promised land. When he thinks he's found it he stops for a while, but not long enough for the fruit to mature. He picks the fruit when it's still green and bitter. And then, disappointed, he throws it away and blames the soil.

And he continues searching for his mirage.

To know how to stop. To savour the present. The reality of life today is my soil, where I can flourish. Lord, don't let me give in to the temptations of 'other places'.

9

If you knew a place where the world's biggest treasure was buried, if you knew that anyone who knew the way could go and help himself to it, and if you also knew that the treasure was life and constant love and joy, could you possibly keep it all a secret?

10

For thirty years I've heard it said, on the subject of the Church as well as the 'outside world': 'We've reached a turning point.' From that I've concluded that we inhabit a mountain whose summit we can only reach by climbing up a corkscrew path. But the most important bend or 'turning point' for each of us at every moment is the one in the process of being negotiated. One landscape is abandoned as another is discovered. Looking below where we've just been, we're amazed at what we've left behind and forgotten, and wish we had appreciated it more. But the truth of the mountain is that its different views and landscapes are all one and the same.

Yearning for the horizons of our youth at every twist of the road can only bring unhappiness. 'It's no longer our mountain,' we complain. We suffer. 'Look what they've done to our mountain.' It's by climbing it that we'll re-discover it and see that it's still the mountain we know and love.

11

I often want to shut my eyes and re-discover You. You're in the house, I'm in the garden. And there I stay because I imagine the trees need me to ripen their fruit. At night, when I enter the house, it's dark and I'm tired. So I go to bed . . . and fall asleep.

12

There are those who have leftist ideas and rightist temperaments. The temperament usually wins out in the end.

13

Who do you speak to? Each person's solitude is inviolable, of course. In each of us there's a bit of mystery that will never be revealed to anyone, not even ourselves. No one can understand man's total dimensions. However great his love, man cannot express it completely.

We cannot know ourselves, or others, except in the light. And we find this light when we search for ourselves, and share what we find with others.

Who do you speak to? It's so much easier to be silent!

14

The longest hours: He works on an assembly line. He explains that the hours aren't of the same length. The first one is 60 minutes long; the second longer; the third even longer; and the last one just goes on and on endlessly. The last ten minutes are eternal, but to gain a little overtime pay, the workers start the line up again. It's dangerous, but they all do it. He does it too. Suddenly, the other day, he realised how alienated he had become. 'I told myself that our devotion to the assembly line equals our love for the Lord.' That same evening, he explained how the requirements of the assembly line even dominated the love lives of the workers. On certain days one was too exhausted even to make love.

More than 10,000 workers near where I live are on assembly

lines, on day shifts and night shifts. For them some men have reinvented slavery, while others are surprised that they're still fighting for shorter working hours and longer paid holidays. As for me, I continue driving around in the car they built for me.

Continue driving, my man, but preach the fight for justice, and never forget that your car is a gift from your brothers. You'll never quite repay them your debt of love.

15

How can you breathe without air?
How can you nourish yourself without bread?
How can you quench your thirst without water?
A breath of air,
A mouthful of bread,
A drop of water
are enough for you, yet you complain that you're not
really living!

'I am your life,' says the Lord.
'Your bread
'Your source
'If you drink of this water you'll never thirst.
'If you eat of this bread you will live forever.'

I suffer from spiritual malnutrition.

16

A few days ago the father of a family said to me: 'I promised my two sons I'd take them on safari in Africa if they passed their final exams. One wasn't keen at all — he had planned something else; the other wasn't too hot on the idea either.'

Today I met a young girl who was in the seventh heaven. 'I passed my exams, so did my brother!' she said exuberantly. 'I must rush, Dad's taking us out to dinner to celebrate.'

What is happiness, and how do you measure it if not by the openness of the heart?

What makes *me* happy?

17

He said: 'I need to know that I'm useful.' I understand him only too well. Who could live without a reason for living? Useless things are usually thrown away.

The best thing I can do for others is to help them discover a purpose to their lives.

I'll never stop believing in people; I'll never stop believing that each one is indispensable and irreplaceable, because he or she is unique. I'll never be attentive enough to others, open to them, silently imploring: I need you, enrich me because until you came along I was poor.

18

Lord, I am no longer afraid of desire.

In the depths of, and even beyond, my being, my desires are born: physical, emotional, spiritual; a desire for boundless love, for communion; a desire to give. I know that in me the breath of love of Him who constantly renews me, projects me towards the world and all my fellow beings. Union, communion and creation through the strength of love.

I welcome the desires in me unconditionally. I will channel then towards my chosen goals and ideals.

I don't want to kill my desires. They are a source, and you, Lord, are present at my source.

19

The emotionally crippled person is always the product of a love gone wrong.

20

We forget that man's liberation in Jesus Christ is the fruit of love and the total 'weakness' of love. This weakness of God's, this self-effacement, offers man the measure of freedom necessary to his loving response, in and by his commitment and struggle; unhappily, it also gives him the opportunity to bury himself in the silence of an agonising desert where, filled with inordinate pride, he imagines that mankind's liberation and the building of the world is his task alone. Man setting himself up as God, eliminating everything that stands in his way. A recipe for chaos. Towers of Babel of societies and civilisations which begin in the crazy hope of building a world of peace and justice once and for all and deteriorate into total confusion, if not bloodbaths. Then anguish sets in; so does the madness of those who are shattered and no longer know how to pick up the pieces and put themselves together again into upright human beings, freely welcoming, giving of themselves, sharing.

21

The day the happiness of others becomes yours,
The day the suffering of others becomes yours,
   You can say that you love.
But it's hard to love — it hurts so much.

22

The beyond — not of time but of people, of objects, of events, of history. My beyond, beyond our moments and actions, that's how far we must penetrate to live reality in all its dimensions. But the beyond is infinite and only prayer allows us to find the way. It is to plunge into the invisible.

What would a tree do without its roots, a river without its source, life without its 'beyond'? It's tragic to live superficially, limited to the thin visible film covering a prodigious invisible reality which so often escapes us.

In my daily life I must strive to be a *man of the beyond.*

23

At a certain point the paths of action and contemplation merge into love. One path validates the other. Yet man's weakness doesn't allow him to follow both at once. A little perseverance would quickly show him that the two are, in fact, inseparable.

24

No situation, no event, no structure can prevent anyone who wants to from becoming more of a person. Man is above such obstacles.

25

Lord, it's wonderful! For two days now I've been 'nourished' by what you allowed me to understand through the work of the Brazilians on the coffee plantations (I talk incessantly about it wherever and whenever I can). Of course I knew, intellectually, that no man can claim to be an island. But I had to think about it deeply for a long time, to see it happening – people working together, needing each other. It took me a while to understand, to really know in my heart . . . I'm glad to be able to write down what I've discovered by your grace.

I'm travelling in southern Brazil. Conferences and meetings in all the major towns and cities. I'm travelling by car or air ferry; yesterday it was a jeep. Four hundred odd kilometres to go. My nice driver chats with me but the drive is long, the heat overwhelming. He falls silent and I admit I'm not sorry. It was quite an effort for me to keep up a conversation. I look out of the window. We are driving past enormous coffee plantations. The workers are many, like bees in a hive. I ask about their wages, work conditions. The answers are horribly disappointing – these workers are in fact suffering, yet they're considered well off compared to the peasants in the north east. My driver goes silent again. I suddenly see myself back in Le Havre with my fellow priests. We're in the dining-room, finishing our good meal with our customary cup of coffee, not realising for one moment that we're drinking the results of the blood and sweat of hundreds of workers. The thousands of kilometres which separate us suddenly vanish. The gaps close. There's no longer an 'over there' or an 'over here'. We're really all the same. My unbridled imagination sees us all bound to each other like parts of a gigantic body; and before my very eyes, a vision grows of a huge moving mass made up of humans dependent on each other.

I look avidly at all these indispensable people. I think of their tools and those who made them. I think of miners extracting minerals from the earth; steel workers melting down their metal and those who turn the metal into objects. I now notice all the trucks on the road transporting sacks of coffee to the port of Santos. I see the factories and warehouses this coffee comes out of, with all the workers inside, from production line workers to engineers. I see dockers loading cargo onto ships; sailors, naval academies, their students, their books and those who print them. I see transit workers in Marseilles and Le Havre, and all the people who keep the ports moving: telephone operators, typists, messengers. I hear the calling and shouting in the Stock Exchange. I see the prices going up and down like yo-yos. I'm present at a union meeting where a strike is being voted on — how many for, how many against? I'm present at the signing of the agreement. I accompany militants who are handing out leaflets and sticking up posters. I follow candidates on the campaign trail; I listen to the cheering and the booing; I count the voices. I'm in parliament listening to speeches, waiting for voting results. I weigh the influence of laws, decrees, regulations. I discover unemployment figures; I observe inflation, foreign trade, the value of the franc, the pound, the dollar. I see everything!!

No, not everything. Because these people I've just passed and who are still working, are in those fields because their parents loved each other, brought them into the world, and because their parents and their parents' parents and so on, right back to the beginning of time, fought, worked, ate, loved. There's no doubt about it, all these people are bound to each other, dependent on each other, enriching or impoverishing, liberating or imprisoning each other. All are tied to economic, social and political structures which they build or destroy, and which allow them to grow and flourish, or slowly waste away.

I had forgotten the land! This land worked by human hands makes coffee grow under the sun. And in eating its fruits, man eats the land. Air, light and water make him grow. I'd forgotten this nourishing earth out of which grow plants and men. I'd forgotten the air, the water, the sun, the moon and the stars.

There are no solitary men, there is a humanity made up of millions of people, dead, alive or yet unborn; all unique and necessary, forming a great mass called the universe.

We are still driving. The sun was beginning to set and the horizon was growing purple. My companion broke his silence: 'Isn't it beautiful!' It was magnificent. That's when I felt the presence of Jesus Christ, as I had done many times before, through his quiet calls, continuous murmuring, or shouts which made me turn towards him — voice without a face, kiss without lips, presence in absence. I knew suddenly that he was there, alive, resurrected, not only in that magnificent sunset but in the life I had just witnessed in the plantations and fields and roadsides. A prodigious history of countless people, loving, supporting or hating each other, but irrevocably bound to each other in solidarity from the beginning to the end of time; multiple parts of an immense body which, through the Saviour our brother Jesus Christ, has become his body.

You are there Lord and I re-join you. When I live with my brothers I live with you. When I fight at their side I fight with you. When I love with them I love with you. Together, with you, we are assembled in a team — the Church — and are building the kingdom of your Father.

'Are you asleep? asked my companion.
'No, I was just thinking.'
Why didn't I tell him I was praying?

26

There's no such thing as a person alone. There are only people bound to each other to the limits of humanity and time.

27

To know yourself is to realise that you're at once unique and multiple.

28

Man is made 'in God's image'. God is a 'subsistent relation'. Within this relationship, man is made; through it, he becomes what he is. Out of it, he falls apart.

29

Total man encompasses all humanity. If he cuts off one or more people, he is impoverished and mutilated. Man grows in communion.

Having reached adult height, man can say in the words of Father de Foucauld that he is a 'universal brother'.

30

A hand is unique, different from an arm or a leg or any other part of the anatomy. But a hand cannot function without an arm, a leg, a heart, a nervous system. All the parts of the body are co-ordinated; each needs the others to live.

If the hand refused the other parts, it would no longer be a hand, and the body would be mutilated.

If the hand accepted the other parts reluctantly, it would suffer, the whole body would suffer.

If the hand wants to be a hand, it must be united harmoniously with all the other parts of the body.

And so it is with man. He is unique. Different from any other but, alone, he cannot *be*.

To know himself, he must know others.

To live and grow, he must not only support others but accept them, both welcoming them and giving of himself freely. He must love all people — that's what Jesus Christ has asked of him.

31

There isn't one person on earth whom I don't need; and I myself am necessary to everyone.

32

My place in the world has two dimensions. Tiny in width ('a drop in the ocean, but the ocean is made up of drops,' as Mother Teresa put it). Infinite in depth.

I can nourish all humanity with life.

33

He who claims he doesn't need anyone is either ignorant or a liar, because he lives thanks to other people who have engendered life since the beginning of time.

If he refuses to live for others, he is a parasite. He grows by feeding off his brothers.

34

I receive life from others — I must give life to others. Every person must be able to give and receive at the same time.

35

Each of my actions, large or small, visible or hidden, has repercussions on all humanity, and for all time, I can enrich humanity, or I can impoverish it.

If I'm open to Jesus Christ by truly loving my brothers, I allow him to come into this world and I can welcome him by welcoming my brothers.

The Incarnation made it possible for men to become the 'sacraments' of Jesus Christ for each other.

36

It was night. I drew the curtains and went to bed.

I switched off the light and was plunged into darkness. I looked at this darkness, thick, impenetrable. Nothing more existed — just me, breathing, oppressed, in the deathly blackness. A moment's anguish. I'm not used to this. I fumble for the light switch and turn on the light.

With a touch of my finger I erase the whole thing.

With a touch of my finger I can bring it all back.

I run my eye over all the objects in the room, happy to be able to see everything again.

Everything is there; nothing escapes me. It is I who become invisible to things and people when I shut myself off in the blackness of my night.

There are no disappeared or 'dear departed' ones here.

37

'It's providential!' I don't like this act of faith, as it's called. It is too often wrongly used. As if God were up there pulling strings like a puppeteer. As if God, like a child with a toy, guided events by remote control. He can, of course, directly intervene in our lives, but if he had to do it all the time he would lose respect for us. Like a lover who is always with the person he loves. God is present in each one of us. He offers us his love. If this love is welcomed, it becomes a force capable of transforming us and doubling our ability to live through events in our lives. So the unexpected, events we can't escape, can be a chance for us to grow, to strengthen us and bear the fruits of life.

We are the ones who, by being receptive to love, make an event 'providential'.

38

The young people I meet today who seriously question are mostly those who have been shocked by the sight of people praying. It's not really surprising — let me explain.

In these modern times, one of the most astonishing sights is that of men and women immobile and deep in prayer, looking radiant and at peace. Either they're crazy (but not to be confused with the immates of a psychiatric ward!) or they have discovered a source of energy, something or someone we cannot see.

But can one be overwhelmed before *nothing*? Can a thirst be quenched in the middle of a desert; can there be enlightenment in a pitch black night; can growth and development take place in space?

If they aren't crazy, then there must be *someone*.

39

I've just been asked to lead a pilgrimage to Turkey 'in the steps of St Paul'. I refused. I'm suspicious of faraway, and attractive, pilgrimages. They hold a hidden danger, a disillusion which is hard to escape. In spite of the good intentions of the organisers, aren't these pilgrimages often, and in varying degrees of course, a sort of spiritual tourism?

I'm told that 'a pilgrimage is demanding and tiring'. Perhaps. But let's be honest: if one had the choice between a trip to Israel, St John of Compostella, Assisi (assuming one could afford it) with the attendant tiring journey and 'demands' of a pilgrimage, and the drudgery of daily life at home taking care of the family, housework and office day in day out, which would one choose?

For myself, if I gave into myself, I would prefer to suffer heat and thirst on the way and let my colleagues bury the parishioners. If I do go off one day, I won't say, 'I'm going on a pilgrimage'; I'll say, 'I'm going on a wonderful journey and I'm going to take advantage of it to pray and meditate a bit more than usual.' I think that would be more 'real' — at least for me.

40

A pilgrimage — a real one — is a long walk in the dusk, sometimes in the night, of daily life. Pilgrims are friends who work together in factories and offices, schools and neighbourhoods, who take time off together, who fight together. A pilgrimage is a walk into the desert with my brothers, with all humanity, towards a promised land, through the history of man's liberation, and for all mankind. There is only one pilgrimage, that of my life bound to the life of my brothers.

41

The vocation (that is, being called to do something) of every person is to love.

The meeting of a boy and a girl is a vocation, a call to love with all one's body, all one's heart. These calls come from the 'other', and through and beyond this 'other', they come from the great Other.

He repeats: 'You shall love (him or her) with all your heart and soul and spirit' *and this love will be the true sign of your love for me.*

42

There's only one language we all understand, the language of love. I have spoken with all the children of the world without knowing their language. We were silent accomplices under the astonished gaze of adults. It's because of my love for children that we could understand each other. The language of love is the language of the Spirit (Pentecost) when man humbles himself to receive it. Then he is understood by all. He who wants to speak 'his' language is not understood at all, and all those around him are dispersed (Babel).

43

R. has just told me that Bernard (a priest and a friend, a wonderful, remarkable, generous man of action who gave his all) has died, defeated by depression. He committed suicide. Stupefied and shattered, I could only think: 'Bernard, why? Why? Tonight I ask myself: 'Why did they let him do it?' *We are all responsible.*

Bernard died exhausted, used up, pushed to his limits, unable to regain control of himself, like a boxer at the end of a fight who can't find his corner in the ring and has to be helped back.

But no one had known, no one had seen, no one had come. Why? Why?

Wounded by the suffering of others and by life's ironies, his vision had clouded a little; crushed by the weight of his own generosity, annihilated by tranquillisers, over-excited by uppers, he couldn't last much longer. What other pressures and harassments did he suffer that we don't know about? I don't know. It no longer matters. What matters now, and what I'm sure of, is that Bernard died because he lacked that little, or large, touch of friendship which dispels lone-

liness and makes a heavy burden seem much lighter for
being shared.

I'm going to the funeral. I had hesitated — why go? For him?
I can pray for him right here. For his family, friends, myself?
Perhaps. However I know that I will be going to very little
more than a show. I can already hear the sudden concert of
unanimous praise and the miraculous disappearance of all
criticism and reservation. Like all sensitive beings, Bernard
wanted a bit of approval, a little encouragement. But he
would have never believed the amount of praise that's going
to be heaped on him now. The tragic thing is that just a
fraction of it could have perhaps saved him. Despite all, I'm
going to the internment. I haven't the courage not to go.

I arrived at the last minute. The sacristy was jam-packed; it
was difficult to get in. Over a hundred priests were there. For
some it was a reunion with old friends. Do we need funerals
to bring us together?
    In the jostling and hub of voices, one has to speak loud to
be heard: 'There you are!' — 'Must be five years since I last
saw you,' — 'You've put on weight.' — What are you up to
these days?' Much noise and smiling, even some laughter.
Now and then, the purpose of this gathering is remembered.
Solemn expressions and whispers. 'Poor old Bernard! Gone,
just like that!' — 'And in such dreadful circumstances,' — 'So
unexpected,' — 'Incomprehensible!'

Where am I?
    Is it that life has got the upper hand here? It is unconscious
relief at finding oneself (since the last funeral) among the
living, the 'escapees'? It is a healthy and robust faith rejoicing
at a friend gone to the kingdom of peace? Is it the super-
ficiality of men temporarily reunited in the same place
without being touched or really united in this mysterious
centre where they are *unique*? Maybe it's all of these things.
Man is such a hotch potch of diamonds and rocks, beautiful
flowers and rotten fruit.
    I had a fierce desire for silence, meditation. Why? To
remember? To feel that I was really suffering to prove the
depth of my friendship for Bernard? What good is this

friendship now . . . useless, dead.

The church was also jam-packed. Places filled half an hour before the service. They were all there — the minister, the newly released prisoners, the general and the ordinary soldier, a soldier, a soldier crying in front of me like a child.

A triumph for Bernard. But it comes too late.

Father D.'s very touching homily restores the essential to my heart, beyond my blind and futile revolt. It's true that a shining light springs out of St Paul's text: baptised in Jesus Christ . . . in his death were we baptised . . . *we are in communion with him through a death similar to his; we will be in communion again through a resurrection similar to his* . . . Christ was defeated by evil but at the heart of this defeat, life sprang triumphant. Bernard too was defeated by evil. He experienced Gethsemane. Perhaps he needed to go that far, to be abandoned by his own: from 'You couldn't stay up with me for one hour,' to the incomprehensible cry, 'Father why have you abandoned me?'

Abandonment. I didn't 'abandon' Bernard. I was faithful in my friendship. But it was a silent friendship. I admired his work, but I never told him so. Why?

Today I found some time for my friend — a whole afternoon. I travelled 200 km for him, and without hesitation. I did it for him, but he's dead. I wouldn't have travelled that far for him had he been alive. Why? Why is friendship expressed in front of a coffin and not in front of a living, breathing person who watches and waits! Crippled people who don't know how to love, to speak, to show feeling. Hearts locked in a hard shell. When will I learn to carry around a living, beating heart?

And when will I learn to truly open myself to God's infinite tenderness. God who wants to reach my brothers through me; *a burning love which has defeated death.*

Bernard, I promise you I'll go and visit the living.

44

The only way to break the chain of violence is to forgive and to love.

He who turns the other cheek is the stronger.

45

Faith is often nothing more than a series of doubts vanquished by love.

46

Noted during a lecture given by Father Bro: 'There were once two doors in a public thoroughfare. Over one door was the inscription: *Paradise.* Over the other: *Lecture on Paradise.* Everyone stood in line for the lecture.'

I'll be even more savage about it: there were probably many priests in the line and at the end of the lecture, they probably pulled out their diaries and fixed a date to meet and discuss it and they took minutes of the meeting and mimeographed them and distributed them and . . . etc.

47

I talked too much again (during a trip). I feel quite drained tonight.

Alone at last! In a quiet room I listen to the silence. I drink it in. I relish it. I feel it in me, penetrating my body through every pore, filling me up, making me whole again. I know that God has slipped into this silence and I join him. I watch him.

Silent God who inhabits me, you who render me whole again and again, I welcome you.

I spoke of you. But did I say too much?

I spent you without counting. But did I overdraw?

One must be silent before you for a long time to earn the right to speak of you. Do I speak of you or do I just create a noise around you — so much noise in people's souls and sensitivity that they can't hear the murmur of your voice?

48

We're like bottles of vintage wine. We are valuable, but if we're shaken, we lose our value.

We must allow our hearts to lie still so that our wine can be good, comforting those who come to drink in friendship.

49

God's principal job is to *make man:* 'Let us make man in our image.' So, to work at 'making man' — developing, helping and protecting him — is to join God in his essential plan, working to realise his project.

50

Praying is 'wasting' time before God. And it is harder to waste time than to give it.

51

To express, or to live, the dualism of mind and body is heresy and sacrilege. We have no right to separate what God has joined. We can attempt this separation in two completely opposite ways: 'reduce' the body to 'free' the mind, or suppress the mind to free the body. Either way, man is broken in two.

52

The body has always been considered beautiful; God wanted it joined to the spirit. Since the coming of Christ, the body has been sacred because God not only came to us in the flesh but, as St John the Evangelist tells us, *made himself flesh.* All human flesh must live out its term right up to the Resurrection, that is, the transfiguration in Christ.

53

The body is not the servant, much less the slave, of the spirit. It is its equal. Man is a 'couple'. When there's a divorce, there's no man and no creation — because it is union in love which engenders life.

54

Many people spend a lot of time looking for new directions. Isn't this just an elegant way of avoiding the road we're on at the moment?

55

When we encounter obstacles in our lives which block the way to whatever admirable and reasonable plan, some of us say 'It's the will of God.' Wrong!

If the obstacles are created by pride, selfishness or stupidity, it isn't the will of God. He is against pride, selfishness and stupidity.

If the plan is just (because God's plan and man's plan shouldn't clash), then one should rest assured that it will be realised — though by some other means. This is why, having fought for and worked hard to get a good project moving, one musn't waste one's efforts, be stubborn or impatient, wanting to see instant results at any price. The goal is important, not the means or the time it takes. Life, when it is *truly* life, always bears fruit.

Redemption is the fruition of the design for life of the Father, by means that he may have foreseen but not demanded. It's failure become success.

56

Accumulated knowledge does not make a wise man. Knowledgeable people are found everywhere, but we are cruelly short of wise people.

57

No man can be completely of this world or rooted in it. If he is a complete man he will be obsessed with nothingness, and with the absolute. All men are transcendental beings. This is man's greatness, and his torment. Man is of the earth, but he surpasses it; and the call of the beyond which is in him is the price he pays for being elevated from his animal condition by the emergence of human conscience, his conscience.

58

To know, to have, to be able. We must fight to bring these to all men. It is grossly unjust that certain people should be systematically shoved aside, but it is vile cowardice and dishonesty to have those who fight believe that the price for their struggle and its success includes their happiness.

59

The other person changes when you change. Start by changing yourself, and the other will follow suit.

60

You don't need a plane to fly you to a desert to find God. It's enough to follow your heart faithfully. But the paths are muddled. At the start you'll probably struggle a lot and stop at mirages. You must learn to walk straight in the shifting sands.

61

By chance the other day I met a lonely, discouraged 'old maid'. I'd heard a lot about her; tiny, quiet, too weak and sickly to take on any work to speak of, but attentive to everyone. She listens and smiles so gently that no one, rich or poor, can resist her.

I tried to make her understand that she wasn't useless, 'nursing the world' as she was, her big heart distilling love drop by drop into the large body of humanity. Many owe her much without realising it. She doesn't know that through her dying people have found hope. I prayed in her name. Perhaps some day I'll send her these lines:

O Lord, I am alone tonight, shrouded in grey,
a prisoner between the walls of my room,
ill at ease with myself, dry as an autumn leaf.
And the dark voice within me surges:
Why are you here, ignored, abandoned?
Others live in twos and threes and fours because they
have engendered life.
Why are you here, ridiculed by so many who think
you barren?
Useless parasite in a world of struggle where the makers
of justice are fighting at the barricades.

You are not alone, says Jesus, because I am with you.
  Silence your dark voice —
  Be silent and listen!
Like you and with you I don't like
  the walls of your room,
  the walls around your body,
  the walls around your life.
You must fight them with all your strength.
But never forget that, despite the walls, your heart is huge
                              and its source fertile.
When you try to love, you can never be useless.
Look at my Mother — she too was alone, ridiculed . . . I say
                    to you, with me she saved the world!
  But she was your Mother too.
  And you are my sister.
  And if I am elsewhere . . .
  I am elsewhere for others, but I am here for you.

  Here I am, Lord,
    Within my walls,
    my body,
    my life.
Buried seed and buried leaven.
Here I am, ready to flower where life has planted me.
Why dream of other gardens? Nothing can grow in the
                              unreality of my dreams.

62

We never finish 'going out into the world', not since our
mothers, through love, pushed us to take our places in life.
We must find our place, occupy it and fill it completely.
Others need us. The appearance of our place in life means
little — what matters is the authenticity and *intensity* of our
presence.

63

Why did I use the word 'grace' when I was talking with C.?
It's been a while since I eliminated 'technical' terms from
my spiritual vocabulary, even current terms which our
parents are familiar with.

C. is an intelligent student, a committed Christian and deeply united to her Lord to whom she prays daily, meditating on his Word. When I mentioned 'grace', she looked puzzled and said, 'What does it mean?' I said: 'It's Christ's love for all of us. When this love reaches us, touches us, it transforms us just like any love does, creating and renewing the person who welcomes it.' 'You should have told me this before,' she answered. 'You of all people shouldn't talk just in technical terms.'

She's right. The butchers of bad theology have in the past sliced up Christ's love and dissected it to death: sanctifying grace, actual grace, attentive grace, this grace, that grace. And we, good students that we are, believed it all and prayed for all manner of graces. We turned Christ's love into an object to be bought at ecclesiastical supermarkets, or ordered directly from heaven where every saint runs his own department.

I'm not denying that theologians need their tools, their methods of analysis, their terminology, but let them keep it all in their laboratories and respect the layman.

It's not up to the people to learn the theologians' language, it's up to the theologians to learn the people's language.

64

It's not surprising that a person who is thrown off, disoriented, from his God (known or unknown) should fall prey to the inextricable mess of his internal vitality – physical, emotional, spiritual. Take away the hub of a bicycle and see what happens to the spokes.

65

Modern man needs to *see* the world he's building. He wants to verify the power of his sciences and his techniques. He wants to stand back and admire the results of his labours. He is therefore not apt to consider a 'spiritual' career. This is one reason why religious vocations have diminished.

The best among the youth want to fight in the workers' struggle; they want to work for less developed countries, devote themselves to fighting poverty and disease. They want to build, but they also want to see their building going up.

On the other hand, there is a shortage of night workers, those who are at the roots and the foundations. Like the sap in a tree they are invisible, until the branch is broken and the sap of a ruined life flows out.

66

When an individual, or a group, lacks love, there has to be another individual, or a group, to compensate by producing *additional love*. Sometimes this extra love is distilled within a struggle.

67

Your eyes, ears, nose and mouth aren't shut doors but open windows. Your skin isn't a piece of armour covering your body — it's a thousand mouths with which to kiss the earth, the water, the sun and the air. You body doesn't stop there — it encompasses the universe.

68

No one can master a situation unless he first consents to do so.

69

I saw the parents smiling peacefully at the burial of their child. 'He's happy,' they said, 'Why should we grieve?' And I heard others comment, 'Aren't they wonderful! Such faith!'

I didn't admire them. I grieved, I felt like crying, even shouting. Jesus grieved over his dead friend.

I fear the person whose dictatorial spirit, without consulting his heart and body, is in command. You can't play at being an angel.

Faced with such things, which we must accept and rightly so, we must slowly come to terms with them, with our body, heart and spirit.

If the mind says Yes, while the heart says No, a profoundly diminishing and disturbing imbalance very quickly and stealthily takes over; and man loses his strength and energy, a lot of it going to nourish a hidden resentment. His heart and mind in conflict, man in fact refuses to accept what has been already decided for him. As long as he's not allowed to express himself in his own way, he'll never be able to 'accept' his tragedies. To use faith to suppress legitimate tears is a sort of crime against one's humanity.

70

She was stretched out on the sunny terrace, her long hair spread out in waves. Whenever she moved, her hair shimmered around her face, a face like a sunlit island in the middle of a dark sea.

I was fascinated. I felt like plunging my fingers into her hair. I felt happy. I let the feeling wash over me gently like the sea.

I am alive. My body is alive. My fingers and my eyes too! Without budging from my place, I drank of this life. I gave thanks. Lord why can't I welcome my desires more often and plunge myself into the pure water without the mud so quickly rising to the surface and slapping out the light?

71

Man needs the kind of love which represents, for him, the face of Christ. Husband, be this face for your wife; wife, be this face for your husband; parents, be this face for your children.

Friends, be the face of Christ for each other; neighbours for your neighbours; and you militants, for those you are fighting with — and against.

As for you, priest, be the face of Christ for everyone.

72

He who applies a rule, a religious tenet, is quickly reassured. If he is faithful in its application he deems himself a good man, and judges those who don't respect the law severely.

He who tries to live the commandment to love takes on a difficult task. Often there are several ways of getting there, and he must pick the one best suited to him. What is even more difficult is that his task will never end, for that is the nature of loving.

73

The path of love is often dark and unlit. You need much faith and humility not to lose your way.

74

Some time ago, an honest and generous working couple came to see me. They both sat in my office weeping silently. Their daughter was on drugs. She had quit her job and gone to live in a commune. The distraught parents didn't know what to do. They had just been to the police to ask for advice and the inspector had sent them to me. They begged me to 'do something'. I struggled a bit – I have not the time or the experience or the means. But I was so touched by their suffering that I gave in.

I met their daughter several times: I also met her friends who seemed happy enough to talk to me. And they certainly talked. During a frank conversation, one of them said abruptly: 'You don't tell these things to a teacher.' Pity the poor teacher – he can 'follow' these youngsters but never meet them on equal terms.

Today I saw the daughter again. I talked to her of her father, of his upright life. She interrupted me: 'That's exactly what I *don't* want – work, home, TV, bed, day in day out for the rest of my life!' And she insisted: 'Yes, I do love my father, but he's a stupid fool, and I don't want to be like him.'

Man's disenchantment with life is increasing everywhere, and the younger generation are more lucid and demanding, wanting reasons for living. Faced with this, adults are lost for an answer.

Today's great deception is an unattainable happiness. Man used to have to fight for himself and his own to secure some material well-being. He chased an object, caught it, possessed it, discovered another he had to have and started all over again. The chase became a veritable race which had him breathless and perspiring, and at the end of his tether. Some stopped running. They realised that happiness did not depend on how many possessions one could acquire.

Their sons and daughters watched them with pity, scorn and revulsion. They didn't want to live that way, but they didn't know how to live, indeed *why* they were living at all.

And we who know the meaning of life have boxed them in. We went along with them, attentive to their problems, supporting their efforts and struggles, but too often forgetting to reveal the goals of their struggling journey. We forgot to temper our actions with good sense.

Today all sorts of voices can be heard in the desert. We won't go on living without a reason for life, they cry. Who will give us a reason?

75

There are days when I feel hungrier than usual. Hungry for everything, for things, for people. I know the reason, Lord. It's because I don't draw enough nourishment from you. So I spend the day, hand outstretched, taking everything I can. In the evening I'm always disappointed. There's nothing left of my harvest — I'm made for giving, and for receiving what others give me, not for taking.

Lord, why should I gather the flowers in my path?
Why rob others of the joy of their colours and graceful
shapes?
Why take them home and imprison them
While they slowly fade and die.

Flowers are for bearing fruit
Flowers are for all to enjoy on the path of life.

My day is over, Lord. Night has fallen.
I gathered many smiles from many faces,
A beautiful bouquet to take home with me
For I was hungry for the look of others.
The smiles faded
The faces paled
The joys died.
In my greedy hands and my selfish heart
My booty failed to turn to honey.

76

I had never been to Algeria before, so I was delighted when I got a chance to visit this proud and painful country, whose wounds were still fresh and stinging.

The first thing that hits me on landing is the dazzling light. A savage sun, as if brand-new, shining fiercely. I drink in the light. I let myself be caressed by the warmth. I want to stroll around, swim and laze in this warm light! It's so inviting, but there are people waiting for me so I must snap out of this premature flight of fancy.

Inside the airport it's quite dark. The light hasn't followed me in — it prefers to stay outside. I can understand that.

I shook hands, said hello, but I didn't really meet the people I was greeting. I was still dazzled by my encounter with that light. I had to pull myself together; I didn't come here to meet the sun but to meet people. Again I realised that you have to have your wits about you to meet people. I must give these souls who've been waiting for me my undivided attention. So I try harder. My handshakes and greetings are no longer empty. But how difficult it is to give yourself as nourishment when you want to pick the fresh fruit in your way for yourself. It's even harder for me at the moment because I've yet to meet one Algerian. The parish I've come to visit is French. There are very few Christian Arabs.

Well, my lad, you can't go choosing your brothers, so be content with the people you're meeting at the moment.

77

The measure of authenticity of my communion with others, and for it to end in love for others, is my capacity for giving my full and undivided attention to those I meet, accidentally or not, chosen or not, expected or not, nice or not, whatever the time and place I meet them in.

78

The first Algerian I had a long conversation with was an elegant, modern, educated young woman. I learned a lot from her, but two things stand out in my mind. First, having asked about her family, I went on to ask her, somewhat timidly, something I was dying to know: 'How did you meet your husband?' The question didn't surprise her. 'My father introduced me to him,' she replied.

'You'd never met before?'

'Just barely.'

'And you didn't hesitate?'

'Absolutely not, since it was my father who'd picked him.'

She seemed sincere. The priest I was staying with, and who knew her family well, confirmed it. He added: 'Things are changing, though, especially in the larger towns. A woman is no longer obliged to marry a man chosen by her father if she doesn't want to. Thank goodness. But to be honest, I must say that in the old days, arranged marriages worked out no better or worse than marriages back home [France].'

Where she has been ridiculed, a woman must at all costs be given back her dignity. It should perhaps also be realised that the roots of love don't lie in trembling bodies or beating hearts, but in the decision — and desire — to make someone else happy, whatever the difficulties, foreseen and unforeseen.

'I don't love you any more,' often means 'I don't feel anything any more, I'm not attracted to you any more.' 'I'm in love with someone else,' often means 'I'm attracted to someone else and I can't help it; I have a desire I can *not* fulfil.'

If loving means only to feel, then man's life is just a rapid succession of sensations.

I then spoke with Mrs X. She works in the offices of a foreign exchange bank. I asked her: 'Are there many of you working here?'

'Several hundred.'

'Algerian?'

'Almost all.'

She added: 'Before the revolution I was the only Algerian woman here.'

'Did your French colleagues all leave?' I asked.

'Yes,' she replied, 'they were gone almost overnight.'

Not convinced, I checked again with my host. He confirmed it. 'And everything works all right?' I asked.

'As well as in France,' he replied.

Many French people who have lived in Algeria — during

and after the revolution — can confirm it too. Of course, there will always be a few who'll scornfully tell you, 'It's gone to the dogs now,' but most people recognise that 'they've' done very well for themselves. So I try to measure how much intelligence, ingenuity and generosity the Algerians must have needed to face a variety of drastic situations from one day to the next, and in all areas. Even it it were an utter shambles, someone said, and it certainly isn't, I would still consider that they're quite wonderful. Think of the time it took to build France! And some people think Algeria can be built in a few years.

79

We've no faith in mankind, and we've too much in ourselves. When a person, or a group of people, has power, he thinks, or convinces himself at any rate, that only he has the right to have and to wield that power.

The best people say they'd like to share it but they feel that the others aren't ready for it yet.

The best of the best say the others aren't ready and want to educate them. But this education seems endless and more demanding than any education they've ever experienced, if indeed they've had any education at all. Will it never end, they wonder.

You can only learn to swim in water. You can only learn how to drive behind the wheel of a car. Power must be shared to be learned.

80

Why must oppressed people so often be forced to resort to violence to seize power, before those in power realise that their greatness lies in sharing, and even at times giving, this power?

81

God gave man power,
Power to dominate and shape the earth,
Power to engender life,

Power to be Godlike in his son Jesus Christ,
Power to build his Kingdom of love within his Church.

82

When people imagine they have a right to power because of
their race or class or culture or creed . . .

When people then wield this power without sharing it
with their brothers, they become lesser men and destroy
themselves.

For man was created in God's image, that is, created to
share, transmit and give power.

83

Tell mankind that power is for all people, but it must be used
for the good of the people.

84

Algiers is a dirty city. Its roofs are in the light, but its feet
are in the dust.

President Boumedienne said to his people: 'When you
spit on the ground, you're spitting on the soil of your
homeland.' I like this pride, this wonderful way of encour-
aging hygiene.

I'm not nationalistic — I feel too much like a citizen of
the world for that — but I find something beautiful in man's
mysterious attachment to his land. Isn't it just the historical
realisation of God's wish? He gave man the whole earth to
cultivate, not as an almighty proprietor with total rights
over it, but as a supervisor who loves and respects it.

Let's not spit on our earth, and if we lie on it, let it be
through love and the desire to enrich it.

85

I've just met Cardinal Duval. I had already been impressed
by him on an earlier occasion. His lucid and courageous
stand during the Algerian war had made him grow in stature.
But when I saw his handsome alabaster face, his long body

encased in red, I wasn't surprised that many had already turned him into a statue and placed him, in his own lifetime, in the gallery of great men of the Church.

He had only spoken a few words to me and I had felt a great distance between us.

Today, in this simple office where he's received me, the monumental statue has descended from its pedestal and come to life before me.

His eyes lit up his whole face; his gentle voice sounded almost timid. This time I had an impression not of force but of great fragility. And yet this is the man who had inspired so much love and hate; who has been kissed, and spat upon. This is the man who had the temerity and courage to speak for justice and freedom, despite threats made against his life. Looking at him, listening to him, I now understand that his strength is not in his stature but in his heart, nourished by the Gospel.

I ask him about the priests in his diocese. I don't understand why so many should have stayed on after Algerian independence. In France there's a shortage of priests, while the ones here seem to have very little to do.

He defends their presence in Algiers vigorously. 'Here, they *are* the Church.'

'But can there be a church without a parish?'

'When two or three gather in the name of Jesus Christ, there is always a church! A priest is always a priest, with or without a parish.'

We have a tendency to reduce the priesthood to a function, turning the priest into a clerk — a privileged one of course because his ministry (that is, his services within the Church) is unique and indispensable. But he's turned into someone who *does*, forgetting the fact that he *is*. Ordination doesn't just confer 'grace' on a priest to go out and act, but marks him deeply and indelibly by uniting him in a very special way to Christ the Priest.

86

I'm not a clerk of the Church, Lord — one who is secure in the knowledge that he has a job for life. I'm not here to distribute the wealth that you amassed for your brothers, carefully placed in the banks of the Holy Spirit where it can gather interest. I'm not your businessman or your accountant — I'm your friend, united with you in a very special friendship which commits me well beyond mere gestures. I'm an actor not a spectator. I'm involved. With you I must live that terrible journey of love you undertook 2,000 years ago and which still continues today.

With you, I must be incarnated, that is, be open to all human life.

I must become a total man.

With you, and in you, I must receive the Father, welcome him and allow myself to be a beloved son.

With you, and in you, my selfish self must suffer and die for love, so as to resurrect permanently.

With you, and in you, I must seal the alliance between the human and the divine, an alliance which will never again be broken.

87

There are no solitary priests in space or time. There are only priests united with their bishop and in Christ. We are together the cornerstone of the Church.

88

We rode for a long time in a jeep. We had to reach the oasis before nightfall. I was going to visit some missionary nuns that evening. It was the first time I had driven in the Sahara desert and I observed the gloomy expanse, flat and dotted with dry forlorn vegetation, with great disappointment. I had imagined majestic sand dunes rippling under a harsh sun. I had wanted the desert to look like all those exotic, romantic photographs and posters one sees of the desert.

To my right I suddenly caught sight of three camels. I nearly broke my neck trying to keep them in sight for as long as possible. It was a first for me — I'd never seen a camel before, at least not in liberty. A little further we saw a whole herd of them with their shepherds who were dressed as colourfully, and as raggedly, as in travel posters. After half an hour, the novelty wore off and they might as well have been a herd of cattle in the fields of my native Normandy for all I noticed. How quickly we get used to things!

We arrived very late, had a quick meal and I went to have my talk with the nuns. The hall was ugly and badly lit. Through the dark windows I could make out a splendid vista of palm trees and sand dunes in the moonlight. This time they were within reach but I couldn't go out there — I had to stay and deliver a talk. I hoped to be able to go and walk around alone for a while afterwards; to look at the desert, to pray (they say you can pray better in the desert...).

The chat lasted a long time. The sisters were happy to have the opportunity to discuss things — very few 'preachers' come to them for they are few and the oasis is out of the way.

When I finally got up, looking forward to my moonlit walk and desert mediation, a young woman who had been sitting quietly at the back came up to me and asked if she could have a word. We spoke for a long time. She had come to visit a nun related to her, and was fighting to break a drug habit. Now and then I thought of the palms, the dunes, the moon and the stars and my desert prayer. They never materialised — instead I ended up saying a short, banal little prayer in a tiny room even uglier than the hall. So I laughed at myself and said to the Lord: 'Why did you lead me to the desert?' It seems to me that he replied, and probably with a smile. 'To teach you not to chase camels when you've got heifers on your doorstep.'

89

I paid a visit to an acquaintance (see No. 43). He was amazed, even embarrassed to see me. 'Oh ... why have you come ... what do you want ...' he stammered. 'Nothing. I've just come to say hello. We haven't seen each other for a long time and I wanted to see you. That's all.'

He was so taken aback you'd have thought I'd punched him in the stomach. We were both a bit embarrassed in fact. We had so lost touch — that simple gesture of dropping in for a visit for no particular reason was now overwhelming. We no longer have the time for friendship!

When I got up to leave, he held me back. 'Wait,' he said

and disappeared for a moment. He returned and handed me a little gift. Now I was embarrassed; it was my turn to stammer. 'But you didn't have to . . . I can't accept this . . . Why? ' Because he just wanted to, that's all.

I thought about it. I know now that it was a voluntary, 'free' gesture — so precious and so rare!

90

Many people today look for silence, solitude and peace. They dream of places where they can rest, away from the daily hassles of living which tear them apart, exhaust them and leave them dissatisfied, wounded and bleeding — and always alone.

But they won't necessarily find peace and quiet waiting for them in other places.

There is a place within us where quiet reigns — the centre, our heart of hearts. There we can find him who is the plenitude of silence. But who will guide us there? We must learn the way.

91

There have been times when I have waited months, and even years, at someone's door.

You can't force you way into a house — it would be breaking and entering.

You must simply be there, like warm sunlight, so that seeing you through the window, the other will want to come out.

You must imitate God's unwavering patience with his children, whom he loves.

. . . But if the other hesitates too long to come out of his fortress, perhaps it is because my light is weak, so weak that it cannot illuminate the way.

92

I have eyes but I don't see. I have hands but I don't touch. I have a nose but I don't smell, a mouth but I don't taste. Because I thought, like so many others, that in order to be spiritual — and this is important — all physical sensations, 'pleasure', were to be held suspect, and even denied. *I have too often atrophied my senses.*

93

It's not a matter of chasing sensations, but welcoming those which come to us legitimately, and directing them towards the goals we aspire to.

94

All our physical needs, all our desires, are good and healthy. But while in an animal they are automatic instincts programmed to perpetuate the species, in man the programme is a guiding spirit. He must seek satisfaction, but in a way and on a level which uphold the dignity of man.

95

The spirit shouldn't dominate the flesh and the heart — it should unite them. And this can only happen if the place, and role, of each are respected, then vigorously channelled towards the common goal — transmission of life (all life, of the body and the heart and the spirit).

96

Love unifies mankind. This mysterious energy permeates man and directs him towards others in a union which will re-create him.

97

Psychosomatic illnesses are illnesses of the soul transmitted to the body; a sick spirit and a healthy body inevitably come into conflict and finally break down.

98

You were separated from your body. Inhabit your body again and together return to life. You and your body must unite and engender life.

99

It seems there are 'souls' that you can't reach unless you go through the doors of the body.

100

Often a man and his life race along separately, never meeting. When that man finally stops in his tracks, old and confined to an armchair or sickbed, his life has disappeared into the horizon. He just no longer has it. Then he can be wise and confident enough to accept things as they are, and finally begin to live. But what kind of life is that?

Stop running. You should be sitting in your armchair because you choose to, not because you're helpless.

101

X. said: 'You have to live your own life.'

'Yes but you should control it, not it you.'

'That's impossible. Nearly everything is imposed on us.'

'One can always fight back.'

'A "prisoner" can't fight back!'

'No one can take away a man's right (unless he's no longer a man) to say yes or no.'

'It doesn't matter whether he says yes or no. He's still shackled.'

'True. Jesus didn't come down from the cross. He could have fought back and let his executioners take his life by force. But just when they thought they were doing precisely that, he gave it freely. No one can prevent man from living his life — and his death.'

102

I was asked to write an article on how we have imposed Western culture on entire populations, and how a 'jazzed-up' gospel should be stripped of all its disguises and once more become a plain little seed to be dropped into fresh earth.

As a rule I don't accept commissions to write. I'm not capable of writing to specification. And even if I were, I

wouldn't be happy at it. My vocation is to live, look and
listen; to carry life and offer it. Whatever filters through into
my simple words I then hope to offer as nourishment to
my brothers.

I wrote the following because I've often thought of the
problems of decolonisation, and also of the Gospel taking
root in other lands and other cultures. Today I marvel at the
harvest to come.

For as the earth makes fresh things grow,
as a garden makes seeds spring up,
so will the Lord Yahweh make both integrity and praise
      spring up in the sight of the nations (Isaiah 61 : 11).

We came to them with our sacks of meal,
Our alphabets and multiplication tables,
And our god neatly packed in a suitcase.
We used the meal to fill their bellies.
We put words in their mouths and our god in their pocket.
We taught them our ways and, like actors on a stage,
                    disguised by make-up,
They mimed the opera of our lives.
We dressed their land in our clothes,
We built towns and devoured their forests,
We built towers that pierced their skies,
We injected civilised blood in their savage veins,
    and offered up this blood, with the blood of Christ,
    on our prefabricated altars.
We came to them rich, but a few poor slipped in amongst us
One by one they discarded their Western clothing and lay
                  naked on the virgin soil.
Then with their bodies bleeding on bodies which were
            bleeding too in the silent night, they united
And rose, walking side by side.
The poor had no words in their mouths,
No gestures in their fingers,
No plans in their heads,
But, hidden in their hearts and their clenched hands, was
                  a seed.
They opened their hands, not to give but to receive,
And from their hands, a few seeds of the Gospel flew away,
    dispersed in the breath of the Spirit.

And from the fertilised earth and bodies, beyond
                    executioners who torture life,
Beyond foolish rebellions that destroy and kill,
Beyond actors discarding, rejecting their masks and
                    crumbling sets
Came spurting forth tiny but tenacious movements of the
                    Gospel, in red, black and yellow
Words of the Gospel in red, black and yellow
Lives of the Gospel in red, black and yellow.
And we watched them, amazed, stupefied, at times
                    frightened.
But one day, when the sun is up, we'll admire, sing and
                    adore their movements and ours,
        their words and ours
        their lives and ours,
        when red and black,
        yellow and white,
together will work to produce the multiform and inexhaust-
                    ible riches of Christ rediscovered forever.

103

No, I can't believe that I'm the author of all these long and
short conversations that are attributed to me. I'm not being
modest, just reasonable. I'm like any other priest. No better,
no *worse* (I emphasise that) than most of them. If anything,
I've met better priests than me. And yet, I must admit that
my life is *apparently* more fruitful than the life of many of
my brothers.

I get hundreds of letters that I can't not read (so I read
them all). I can't refuse to listen to the hundreds of people
I've met in the four corners of the world who say: 'I read
such and such a book of yours — I saw you on TV — I heard
you talk — it changed my life — I was overwhelmed . . .!' I
take it all in, and I say thank you. What else can I do? At
first, I was embarrassed with all this attention; I would be
evasive, but before long, I decided it was ridiculous to feel
this way. After a successful lecture tour or the publication
of one of my books, for example, I would be afraid to be
happy. I thought it was a form of vanity to be happy about
these things. Today I acquiesce and rejoice quietly. When I'm

told that I'm well known overseas, or that my books total millions of copies, and how wonderful it all is, I answer that yes, it's quite wonderful. I'm not going to pretend otherwise, or give in to false modesty and meaningless protestations of 'Don't exaggerate! It's nothing!' Not being self-effacing, I probably lose my halo in some people's eyes. Well, that's too bad. As it happens I don't have a halo — I mean the real thing, an aureole of light — so I certainly don't want to be given a plastic one off some statue! So, with or without a halo, as the client wishes, I let myself be photographed.

It would be unfair to say that I do all the work — I don't, and it would be impossible anyway. I may speak to millions, but one friend thinks and says the very same things if only to a couple of hundred parishioners. I may have my works published, but another friend photocopies his for a couple of dozen readers.

Who does the work, touches hearts, changes lives? God, of course. But this is too simple an answer. God wants to need us — I did say 'us', all of us. So, who does the work, touches hearts and changes lives? My friend, the one who talks to one or two hundred parishioners; my friend, the one who writes for a dozen or so readers; and all the people who don't speak or write but who, without exception, are doing their jobs and doing them well, whether for one person or thousands.

I am certain that all I do is to harvest what others have sown. Anonymous lives have fertilised my tree and nourished my roots; and the sap of my words is but the blood of others. I know some of the blood donors; I know their lives and the extent of their love. There are many many more I don't know of, but I do know they exist because you need a lot of seeds to make a harvest.

Energy isn't noisy and sap isn't visible. Only the flowers and fruit can be photographed. I often represent these flowers and fruit, but their energy is elsewhere — it doesn't come from me. I only have a little, no more than anyone else.

My thanks to you, unknown brothers who bring me all this nourishment in the night. Tomorrow you will have your due recognition — your name on posters, the flashing of cameras, photographs and applause, and the numerous thank-yous which I get but which are all for you. I accept them and hold them on your behalf. They don't really belong to me.

And I go on calmly letting myself be photographed. I keep the photos. I will show them to you, I promise, and you'll be stunned to see your face in them.

104

It is dangerous to be the one who harvests.

105

You can confide your failures to your friends. They'll listen, comfort and support you.

You can confide a small success to your friends. They'll be happy for you.

But if you triumph, then you must ask to be forgiven.

106

People often put me on a pedestal and say: 'You're a celebrity!' But I know that underneath the celebrity is a simple, naked man.

107

Tell me what you own and what you don't have.

What is there you'd want to keep?

What right do you have to capitalise when you know that your brothers live and depend on what they receive from others, including you?

Living is to constantly welcome life, and give it.

If I cling to my life, I deviate from its purpose.

If I cling to my life, I stifle it, because it is made to move from me towards others.

If I cling to my life, I stifle the others who need the life I must pass on to them. I commit a 'mortal' sin.

108

Some days I find myself so tense, with my shoulders hunched up as if they had been carrying a heavy load. What unknown baggage do I unconsciously carry — all my worries, suffering, anguish . . . and everybody else's?

Why have I turned myself into a full-time docker working on the world's quays? Why go through life carrying loads which leave me drained and surprised that fatigue can reach such proportions? I know it's not physical; it's a tiredness of the heart. I'm like a weight-lifter, lifting heavier and heavier weights. I should have offered them to the Lord; above all, I should have welcomed the weight of infinite love, the love that the Lord carried to the cross.

But you, unhappy man, cannot even carry your little daily cross.

109

Religious practice and the practice of the Gospel should not be confused. The first can be measured, but the second can't. The second is the sure way to 'heaven', but the first . . .?

110

Once again, I've been aggressive in discussion. It's a sign of incompetence, fear and pride. Whatever the cause, though, it's a *failure*, especially as I managed to silence the person I was talking to. It's the worst kind of cowardice to cause someone to become incapable of fighting back. It's refusing the challenge, and a sign of weakness hiding behind a façade of strength. A strong person is one who allows the other to participate; one who listens and understands the other's point of view. Like a psychologist who listens and says, 'If I understand you well, what you're saying is . . .', and you reply, 'Yes, that's exactly what I mean.' Once I've truly understood the other, then I can voice my opinions.

111

I fled to a retreat one week-end to get some peace and quiet. After lunch, I decided to have a nap, but the people around me started asking me questions. What else could I do but try and stay awake and answer them. I had come to be silent, but I was obliged to speak. I did it against my will, and it showed, because my heart was yawning, if not my mouth. I thought at the time that they couldn't have thought much of me.

Tonight I tell myself. 'Once again you failed to love.'

It's definitely much easier to dream your life than to live it.

112

Once again the discussion centred on X.'s accomplishments in a certain matter. Despite my good intentions, I had to make an effort to stay calm. I've lost count of the times this subject's been brought up 'for discussion', to make us 'think'. I couldn't help likening it to a piece of chewing gum that you can chew forever without wearing it out — it activates the saliva but imparts absolutely no nutrition.

You have to *look* at life. To be precise, and effective, you must reflect on it for a moment: an event, an action, a fact. You must 'see, judge, act' — this is the unique and wonderful maxim held by the *Action Catholique*, a system that they teach. But like all systems, it becomes paralysing and destructive in the hands of narrow-minded people, or people who get too used to it. The instigators of such a system or method begin to see their evangelical drive peter out, their adherents getting sparser and the whole thing becoming too complicated and academic. So, in the midst of all this, some 'militant' starts a 'new movement' and he gets talked about and told what a fantastic thing it is he's doing (others have done the same, but nobody's noticed it, not even the results) and the heavy machine begins rolling. Discussion, reflection, analysis, reports, dissection, more discussion, more endless analysing at every conceivable level — local, regional, national. The 'movement' begins to acquire fantastic dimensions; its consequences multiply prodigiously. At the end of the road, the person who started it all can hardly recognise his own idea, the subject of monographs, proclaimed in meetings, written up in bulletins and newsletters. Dozens of people will have exchanged views and discussed the thing to death. Like parasites they will have fed off one person and then retired, satiated, waiting for someone else to start up something so that they can start analysing and reflecting all over again. How intensely they bore me! And here I am wasting my time getting furious over it.

Come to think about it, it's just as well no one reads my private notes, because somewhere there's bound to be someone who'd say, 'Your intense boredom says something to me; why don't we discuss it and . . .'

113

This morning I rediscovered the extraordinary power of love at the bedside of a dying man.

I sat there not knowing what to say — what can anyone say to a dying man? I watched him. I thought him ugly, this old man with a face ravaged by wrinkles, oily with perspiration, where who knows what mysterious bombardments had dug those red and black craters in the stubble of his beard.

His wife held his hand as he lay there motionless. She leaned over him: 'My dearest, the father's here to say hello.' Then, as if she had forgotten my presence, she caressed the old man tenderly. 'My love, my beautiful love,' she whispered. I was a little embarrassed and taken aback by her words. How could anyone be so blind, I thought. No doubt about it, love was blind!

Then something extraordinary happened. Responding to his wife's tenderness, the old man opened his eyes and a pale, tremulous smile hovered across his lips — a smile that was like the sun trying to pierce through dark clouds. He looked at his wife for a long time, then the clouds dispersed as he smiled widely, his whole face glowing. Then I saw it. I saw what she had been seeing all along. *He was handsome!* She was right, oh so right! Love isn't blind. On the contrary, love lets you see what others don't. It lets you see beyond the physical person, lets you see his real self, unique; as only those who love each other can see, know and admire.

114

I thought he was a sociable type because he always wanted to meet lots of people. But I soon realised that it was only so that he could talk about himself.

115

It took a long time for me to understand why some young people who talk to me openly about themselves, and look to me for guidance, also admit to being timid in my company. 'You're always giving, but we have nothing to give you in return,' they say. I do realise that unconsciously I put them in a position of poverty, perhaps even of beggars; and it's always humiliating to go asking when you think you have nothing to offer in return.

Loving means giving, but also receiving. Sometimes it's easier to give because you're in control, like a rich man giving handouts to the poor.

I don't dare tell these youngsters that whatever they may think, they offer me much in return. Is it because I'm afraid they won't understand? Or is it because it's hard to reveal things we hold intimate? They don't know that I have a profound need for them. They give me what no one else can. By coming to me, by needing me, they allow me to have the children I never had, children I gave up by choice, and for them.

116

You must give others the opportunity to give — otherwise you are paternalistic and not a father.

117

God gives us all so that we can give him all in return. This is what is called 'giving thanks' — voluntarily giving in return to the Father all the riches he has bestowed on us. Because the Father gave us his Son, because the Son gave us himself, we can all together offer the Eucharist — the supreme gift, the one that saves the world.

118

I've just been listening to a young Korean violinist on television. A truly magnificent talent! I've never been so moved by anyone's music.

I think of a human violin, strings vibrating like a human heart, in love with its violinist, the two marrying and their embrace making music for others.

I am that violin when, loving and open, I offer myself to you, Lord, you who mysteriously play my life. But I am also often an inert wooden bow in your hands, my broken strings avoiding your searching fingers.

Lord, why do I let you play my life without singing with
you?
Your harmony becomes dissonance when it crosses my
rebellious flesh and heart.
Tonight I come before you, before your life,
I want to be one with your love, your love which has
created me.
I want to be the music that you whisper in man's ear,
The music that is heard in the four corners of the world!

119

I return home alone. The house is empty. Silence and the night.

I had a wonderful evening. Forty or fifty young people talking, discussing, singing. They wanted to go on forever. They never want these evenings to end. They love these moments of relaxation and joy. Me too. I'm there among them, happy that they're happy. I'm silent. They must think me a very quiet person. I don't feel like talking. I watch them. I see them.

I see everything — the sad look when a certain song is sung (and I know why); a sensitive gesture towards an isolated newcomer; the sharing, the needing, the wanting; the closed eyes seeking to meet their Lord. I also see all the looks and smiles weaving invisible ties throbbing with life . . . Children of my heart!

Some of them are already in love and will make their lives together. Others have made mistakes which they have yet to realise — and they will, in their own time. And there are others who haven't even discovered each other yet. I wait, knowing that the spark will appear sooner or later, and my eyes will tell it to my heart.

This evening, X. (who's in love) leaned over and whispered, 'I never thought I could be so happy.' I watched them all, leaning against each other shyly. They were beautiful, radiant. I was happy for them and I, too, thought, 'I never thought I could be so happy . . . for the happiness of others.' Once again I realised that in me suffering and great joy live side by side. I don't regret having dedicated my life to other people, giving myself up for the love of mankind — but I'll never get used to the sacrifice of it, and I will always feel a tightening in my heart when I see and marvel at the love around me, blossoming and bearing fruit.

What do they really think of us, those who observe us parish priests and are scandalised, mocking, pitying or admiring? Do they think that it's a simple matter of making a definitive choice, having a vocation, therefore we must be made for that sort of thing, with no problems, mistakes or failures? They have no idea that our love, like any other, has to be built daily, in darkness or light, in suffering or joy.

Tonight I am alone. Children of my heart, I write this for you.

Children of my heart
I saw you in love, my children
I saw the looks, the smiles that passed between you
I saw your eyes say 'yes' before the word even reached
your lips
I saw your hands search out other hands, joining, inter-
twining.
I saw your fingers play on other fingers as on the strings
of a guitar.
I saw your bodies tremble and float towards each other
like the sails of a ship coming into port.
I saw your mop of curly hair, my child, rest in the crook
of his arm
And I saw both of you laugh, pout, and laugh again.
I saw you searching for the way, already suffering, at
times crying.

Children of my heart, I saw you in love,
your love always bringing out mine,
the joy of your joy in my wide open heart.

But you don't know, cruel and precious children,
   that this joy has touched me so deeply that it has created
   a strange and wonderful wound —
Sweet and gentle, burning and bleeding
The wound that long ago gave me the kiss that set my life
                                           on its course.

Did you know, children of my heart
That I too am loved?
My lover is called 'love' and I love my 'love'.
But my love makes me suffer, for it is so often hidden
                                                   from me.
When I look at you, beloved children,
I look for its face.
And sometimes I would like its face to resemble yours,
                                               little girl.
But my lover has no face, I know it, I accept it.
And yet, again tonight I grope around in my darkness,
   my lips seeking its lips
And I suffer in silence
I suffer — and I bleed.

Children of my heart, tomorrow I'll tell you only of my joy,
   my joy for your joy, not of my wounds
And you won't know that the red roses I'm offering the
                                       Lord on your behalf
Are in truth drops of blood.

120

Some people really believe I love them. Others guess that I
love them. Many don't even suspect how far this love can
go. Some doubt me and, horrors, wonder if I love them only
because it's my duty. Finally, others think it's impossible to
cherish so many children at once. They don't seem to know
that if a heart is *open* to infinite love, it can love infinitely.

I can understand parents who love a newborn child without taking anything away from their other children. They
love each child individually and completely, taking nothing
away from any of them.

I can also understand you a little better, Lord, you who

love all your brothers, giving yourself entirely and equally to all. And I also understand that to love the way you do, one must take up the cross. Unknowingly, my heart's children present me with this cross when they bring me their love. It's up to me to grasp the cross – and at the same time to be willing to carry it.

It's so difficult, and yet, Lord, if I can help them love a bit better, I'm willing to give you my life ten times, a hundred times over, as many times as necessary to share something of the love you bear them.

121

Because their *ideas* are progressive, because they think very hard about revolution and changing society, because they talk about it a lot, because they vote for the Left (at least, they say they do, but they don't always), because they join some demonstration or get involved in some movement, they think they've done it all. They judge others harshly, call them 'bourgeois' and condemn them. But in the things that affect them directly – their jobs, their cars, their comforts, the future of their children, their homes – they behave just like the people they label 'bourgeois'.

They think leftist ideas but live rightist ones. They are not the stuff revolutions are made of.

122

He specialises in 'unbelief'. He sets up commissions on unbelief. He organises sessions on unbelief. Many sign up for them. They study unbelief, they pursue it, measure it, dissect it. Such a fascinating subject!

The 'specialist' is convinced and convincing. His subscribers are many. He's a real apostle of unbelief. We were blind, now we can see. We have become unbelievers. They're everywhere and we didn't know it. There are even some unbelievers who hide behind a mask of belief which can in itself be a form of unbelief. We need more people to take up the cause! Fortunately there are a few who have the vocation; they will dedicate their lives to unbelief. . . . In short, it's a success. The subject mobilises many people who can study, reflect and discuss so well that these beautiful people ... no longer have the time to proclaim Jesus Christ.

123

Nothing is more difficult than writing simply. I'm not the first to have realised this! In any case, I keep on experimenting. I have to rewrite continuously to try and eliminate clutter and be more precise. Clarity doesn't allow cheating. A heavy style and lots of big words obscure the subject, and make it sound more profound than it really is. And that's a much easier thing to do. And yet, what is simpler and more profound than to write: God is Love?

When I write just for myself, I like to play with words and style. But when I write for others, I don't want my words to sound seductive, like a girl whispering 'Come along darling' to the reader.

124

What good is your word if, when given to another, it doesn't become part of him? (And the Word was made flesh and lived among us.)

125

You've got to stop and look at the other person. You've got to give him the chance to be what he is. Look at him, admire him, welcome him — gratuitously, unconditionally.

'But sometimes they say I'm too quiet.'

'No, you still talk too fast.'

'But he's come to listen to me!'

'True, but he's come to listen to you talk about *him*. He's come to see his image reflected back to him, more clearly, more precisely. When he comes to you, he's the one who wants to talk.'

'But what if he doesn't talk?'

'His silence is a form of speech.'

'And if he persists in staying silent?'

'Then you must patiently offer him a few words that he can use to express his thoughts to you.'

126

From what I can see, groups, movements and organisations suffer from three unhealthy elements. First, the group grows and develops (or engenders itself, somewhat like giving birth to a child). Second, the administrative staff proliferates while their members diminish. It's an illusion to think that if there is no basic demand, *born of a real need*, for the organisation in question, it can be induced by electing and appointing agents and officers. Third is when 'technique' overtakes 'mystique' (Charles Péguy in his time had already remarked on this erosion). The more the latter loses its vitality, the more methods and techniques are developed and perfected. These don't work anyway — they only demand and ultimately sap the energies of the administrators. It becomes a vicious circle, and requires a courageous reappraisal — not at the top, but by a return to grass roots.

127

This morning I accompanied Father Lebret (a Dominican and founder of *Economie et Humanisme*) to the ship. He is sailing for Peru on the invitation of the republic's president. The president has asked him to do a study on a development plan for the country. We discussed the project for two good hours. It was a live and enriching discussion, but what was even more enriching was Father Lebret's attitude.

Just before we left for the quays, a young JOC member came to my office. I told him I was too busy to chat, and paused at my desk to sign some letters before setting off. When I rejoined Father Lebret, there he was sitting on the landing, deep in conversation with the young man. I listened and watched. Father Lebret was looking intensely at him, devouring him with his eyes; in fact, eyes which seemed to be a repository for all the mischief in the world and, at the same time, intelligence, lucidity and goodness; eyes which scrutinise and, as if impatient to see deeply, look lively over the spectacles perched on the end of his nose. Those eyes are 'listening'.

It was getting late. I interrupted: 'Father, the ship's captain is waiting for you!' 'Yes, yes, I'm coming,' he said.

But he asked the boy another question, listened to his answer, asked him yet another ... I waited for about half an hour. When we finally drove off, he sighed, 'That was so interesting. I wish we'd had more time.'

We got to the ship quite late. A porter took Father's luggage to his cabin. An officer came up: 'Father Lebret? Welcome aboard. Pleased to meet you ...' Pleasantries back and forth. Meanwhile the porter had disappeared and Father Lebret, tip in hand, chased after him. He went one way and despatched me another. Embarrassed, I asked the officer to find the porter. Fifteen minutes later there was still no sign of him. Father Lebret was upset. I said timidly, 'Father, they're waiting for you,' but he wouldn't budge. Finally he saw another porter and called him over. 'Excuse me, my friend,' he said, 'one of your friends carried my luggage and took off before I could give him his tip. If you see him, could you tell him I'm terribly sorry and give him this money. If not, keep it for yourself.' The porter was dumbfounded, the officer didn't seem to understand what was going on, and I could only admire this man, this United Nations international expert whom heads of state consult, advisor to Pope Paul VI (we owe part of the encyclical *Populorum Progressio* to him), author of several development projects for whole countries, regions and towns. Oh yes, I admired this man who can not only be interested in the world's leaders but also in a simple young man on my doorstep, and who can waste half an hour for the sake of a friendly gesture. People like him can change the world.

128

I still judge people too quickly in conversations and discussions. However, I think this is just a superficial attitude. In fact, I feel quite small before others. I condemn actions, not people. I can see too well what motivates them not to understand all the things that have brought them to such and such a statement, thought or action.

Man is millions of years old. Who could know him? Who could judge him? To know him you would have to judge all the people who came before him and made him what he is today.

129

Who made you? Your father and your mother, and their parents and their parents' parents, and all the mothers and fathers before them.

What made you? The bread you ate, that your parents ate, that their parents and everybody's parents ate. . .

What made you? The kiss they gave you, the one they received. The slap they gave you, the one they received. The lesson you learned, the one they learned. Your prayer, their prayer.

Who made you? Your friends and theirs. Your enemies and theirs.

What made you? The place where you lived and where they lived. The work you did and the work they did. The laws that govern you and govern them.

What made you? All the yeses and noes that you uttered and the chains of yeses and noes which were uttered before you since the first man.

What made you? The sun, the rain and the stars.

Who made you? All men on earth, the universe, the good and the evil.

What made you? The breath of Him who said, 'Let us make man in our image.' The breath of Him who creates man daily by loving him.

How could I judge you? How could I possibly weigh the value of bread, of smiles, of blows. How could I count the rays of the sun and all the rain drops? How could I measure the depth of good and evil, the suffering and joy, the substance of prayer? Oh man, I cannot but accept you and welcome you *as you are*, now, today, for me, for everyone.

You are too deep a mystery for me to fathom, and I can only see you in the light.

Man, as immense as the universe itself, as large as humanity and time. How big you are!

130

(In Lebanon)
This afternoon I met a very old Maronite monk. I was told he spoke Aramaic fluently, with the same accent as Jesus.

I was startled — were they having me on? I wondered. I asked him to recite the Lord's Prayer in that language. I listened to him with my eyes shut? Was I being romantic, or what? Well, perhaps, but it also had to do with my faith: driving around all day on the roads that Jesus had walked, I asked myself if I really believed in the Incarnation. God with us, in Jesus Christ, on this earth, in a particular geographical location, in a precise historical context!

O Lord, increase my faith.

131

To reach its destination, the whole train must move. Without its engine, a train can only sit motionless in the station.

All dough becomes bread, but without yeast, it remains motionless in the kneading-trough.

There are many carriages but few engines; much dough but little yeast. The danger we face is of trains sitting permanently in railway stations and bread dough never leaving the kneading trough.

132

It's not a question of 'giving to charity' or 'making love'. True love and charity exist anyway, they don't have to be given or made.

It's rather a question of 'being' love, 'being' charity, that is, completely giving and welcoming before Christ and all men.

133

Once more I've seen how, when the lack of love has destroyed a young person, only supplementary love can make up for the loss — that is, one and a half times the amount normally needed. But why must the price be so high? Where only a little was needed, now an awful lot must be given if any good is to be done.

How many times, while trying to gather this huge ransom of love, I've seen that it could never be fully met. Not loving is one of the greatest sins, and only an infinite love can fill the void of a failed one.

Human love isn't enough. There must also be the love of God. That's what redemption is all about.

134

I'm not saying 'God exists, I've met him,' but 'God exists, he has embraced me.' I'm still sustained by those few deeply moving encounters with God in which he touched me, and marked me incurably. Anyone who hasn't been gripped by such an encounter and held his breath in the embrace of God, can't live his life for God and in the service of his brothers.

I will never regret the seminary which, despite the stupidity of certain rules and regulations, offered me a long sojourn in the desert — where silence and simplicity encourage encounters with God.

Is it an illusion? Over-reaction? No, not if the encounter results in a lifetime commitment.

What proves the authenticity of such encounters? The strength they give one to live in the service of others, demanding nothing in return.

135

The primary messenger of life is the body. It says to another 'I love you,' with a smile, a look, a gesture, lips and words. When it wants to say it completely and without reserve, it says it in a strong embrace. And it is only the beginning of a long song which must grow deeper, beyond, well beyond its limits, in the silence and the night. But why are we so often dependent on this poor limited body, getting older every day? Why do we need flesh on flesh to express what infinitely surpasses the flesh?

The body is too small and too narrow. Its song is much too big for it; so the body vibrates but cannot sing. All it can do is sigh, moan, and sometimes shout. It imprisons us for we are too dependent on it. The body is essential and beautiful but limiting. And whoever stops at the body will never know love beyond a quiver or two.

I would like to show people that life is more than a look, more than a kiss, more than an embrace, that love is music echoing into the infinite, even when the instrument has stopped playing.

136

A priest is not a man who refuses to give his body. Like all my brothers I have to give myself entirely: *body*, heart, soul. But how do I do it?

You, Lord, you found the way. You give your body in the bread and wine of the Eucharist, and you will continue to give it to the end of time. But what about me? I must give my body, but I can't offer it in an embrace. If I could, then I too could share it to the end of time.

I give my body when I rise, dead tired, and push it to go to a meeting.

I give my body when I offer my undivided attention, my actions, my words.

I give my body when, day by day, year after year, I try to keep it available to offer it, with my soul, to whoever needs me.

When my body becomes too old to move, when it is lying still on a bed, incapable of answering the soul's call or the heart's desire, I hope then to have the courage to offer up its suffering and its diminishing light . . . give my body for the last time to the earth it came from . . . and wait for my Lord to come for me.

137

I've been in Rhodesia for about ten days now. I've done nothing but talk — to small groups, large gatherings, youngsters, adults. But they're all Whites. When am I going to meet the Blacks? I can't even see any around! Where are they? . . . I've done it, and I'm shattered.

When I crossed the line into the Black section, I was startled by the extraordinary swarming mass of people. I felt as if I had crossed the threshold into life. Nowhere else had I encountered such impressive people, brimming with strength and vigour. And I felt deep down that these people would triumph one day, but not before the blood of their martyrs had been shed. One has to be blind not to see it. Where do the Whites get the crazy idea that they can indefinitely oppress and control the lives of others?

I was taken to a huge church in a Salisbury suburb. There I

saw two or three thousand Blacks crowded in the pews, sitting in the aisles, in the choir, on the steps of the pulpit, everywhere. They had come from the surrounding region as well as that section of town. Of different religions, they were accompanied by their pastors and ministers. It was extremely hot.

I talked for a long time. I had been told to take my time. A student translated what I said into *shona*, their main langauge. It was his first time and he was proud. And in spite of the heat, the slowness of the translation and the relative discomfort, they listened, motionless. The silence was impressive. When babies cried they were quickly hushed at their mother's breast.

I said none of the things I had planned to say. Instead I wanted to answer the questions that had been put to me before entering the church. I had been asked why I'd come all this way, I, an 'important' person, why come here when I surely had more important things to do . . . and, wasn't I afraid?

I came, I said, because I needed you. I didn't know you and I wanted to meet you. I need you. Without you I am incomplete, a body without arms or legs.

They were visibly astonished at my words, and they said as much afterwards. I was sincere, and very happy to see them, to hear them sing, to look at them, to talk with them, to listen to them. They understood this. They felt it. They were essential to me, as they are essential to all humanity and to God. I told them that not only I (for I was of secondary importance) but the Church needed them. That we were one people, a community, where each had his place, his role and that together we constituted the great body of Christ. Then I was able to tell them that if we Whites needed them, they too needed us; and when they had finally broken the chains of the criminal bondage we had forced on them, when they were finally freed from our oppression, not to reject us! Because if they did, they in turn would be spiritually mutilated and bereft of Christ.

Outside, in the huge grounds of the church, they sang and danced for a long time. I was told it was their way of thanking me for what I had said.

138

There are silences that are a form of repression, a communal pit full of words and cries festering in carapaced hearts.

There are silences that are resignation, sluggishness and lassitude — rear-guard defences where we retreat, defeated, trying to hide the fact that we are retreating.

There are silences inhabited by noise.

Silences which are ramparts against others, entrance forbidden.

There are silences which are
> welcome,
> respect of the other,
> communion,
> adoration.

There are silences where silence reigns supreme —
> silences inhabited by love,
> on whose fringes God appears.

I often crave silence — but which kind?

139

To be assured of his existence, man needs recognition. More often he needs admiration. Now there is in every man, whether or not he is devoid of any intelligence, whether or not he is completely insignificant or a great sinner, a little part of himself, a little moment in his life, which is admirable. It just needs to be discovered and highlighted.

140

The silence of God weighs on men like a dead-weight. Even today I listened to the bitter complaints of some people who feel this weight. I understand how they feel because I often feel that way myself. This evening, in the face of their suffering, I also suffer.

> Why are you hidden, Lord?
> Why do you hide in this grey day where my work weighs on me like a punishment?
> Why do you hide in my untidy house where everything has to be put into place daily?

Why do you hide in our worn-out love, love
  like stagnant water whose source has dried up?
Why do you hide in this body which calls to me,
  flesh wanting my own hungry flesh?
Why do you hide in the sickness of my body,
  faithful suffering, unwanted spouse?
Why do you hide in my human struggles
  when I am fighting with and for my brothers?
Why do you remain hidden, you who came to this earth,
  You who spoke so forcefully,
  You who wept so piteously?
Why do you hide in the night — my obsession —
  the night that falls after sundown
  the night flowing in my heart like approaching death.
Why do you hide, Lord, why?
Speak to me Lord!
Dear Lord, why do you hide when *I know that you
                                              are there.*

141

I'm very pleased to have met Martin Gray the author. We discussed the subject of the sanctity and protection of life at a large gathering in Montreal. That same evening we found ourselves sitting next to each other at a dinner given by the mayor of Montreal. We got quite friendly. Despite facial scars (the result of torture) he is an attractive man. True attractiveness doesn't depend on the physical. At the same time, I felt slightly uneasy in his presence. I had read his books and knew him by reputation — was it because I feared he wouldn't live up to the image I had of him? What if he turned out to be just like anyone else! We need heroes and supermen we can look up to, to help us believe that we have hidden strengths beyond our imagination. Now here he was, in person, and I was afraid he wouldn't live up to his image; and I was afraid of being disappointed.

There was no time, and it wasn't the place, to talk too seriously. We didn't really get to know each other well enough. I must accept his invitation to his place in the south of France some day; I want to tell Martin Gray to continue being Martin Gray with all his strength.

142

There are people who take on a personality that isn't theirs. They are no longer themselves, not even in their own eyes. They have lost themselves. Much of the time, however, it is others who make us out to be something we're not, and it's very difficult to escape the image they've created of us.

143

At times it seems as if there are less and less effective people working in the Church, and that the Church is more and more obliged to fall back on itself, and be dependent on a small, detached community.

During a brief visit in a large town, I was invited to attend a service where a nun was to make her simple vows. In the congregation's 'private' chapel were two bishops, twenty priests, an army of nuns and a few lay people. We all found good reasons to be there. Myself, I didn't dare refuse to attend; I had some free time before a lecture I was to deliver. But really, have we nothing better to do than trot out here this morning, I wondered. Are there really so many priests and nuns out there? And don't a parish nun's vows concern all the Christian community? That being the case, why is it being held in private?

Everyone present was an 'official'. They were quite old; but the songs were young, just like some of the nuns — young, but dressed in black. I got an overall impression of old age huddled up in a cold, dim corner. Old men gathered together at someone's deathbed. A dying race whose few great grandchildren, present there that day, offered little hope for its survival. These congregations will either open up to the flame of the Holy Spirit and rise from their ashes, or they will die.

144

Seated opposite me in a train, a young girl cries silently.
  Beautiful child, why are you crying?
  Why is this sudden black cloud passing over you?
  Your eyes are too bright — are you crying inside?

Why?
It's a mystery; I'll never know what's tearing you up inside.

Are you hurt physically?
Or is it your heart that's aching.
Has your love left you? Are your burdens too heavy?

I'll never know anything about you
You'll never know anything about me.
Our eyes barely met.

But you were there before me, beautiful child.
For one second I saw your cool body
A fruit for the parched.
But I have no right to pluck the fruit that peep down from
the high walls of my journey.
That fruit is yours alone, it is your life, shining beyond
mere flesh
I see your essence like a wound.

Resigned to the sleep in my eyes and the emptiness of
my hands
I continued on my journey
And without seeing you or touching you
I rejoined you, sweet child before me.
It was 'You'.
Gently, silently, I dressed your wound, I brushed your
tears away and held you in my arms
And offered you to God who is *my* love.

When I reopened my eyes
Your own were dry, beautiful child.
The cloud had lifted and Spring was all around you,
You were sleeping.

Beautiful child before me, sleep in peace.
I will rock your cradle with my love.

145

God allows me to become God (in Jesus Christ) yet often
all I want is to become a man.

146

I went to see her this afternoon. She must have been in her late seventies. She's an invalid, living alone in a sad two-roomed flat. She has no family to speak of. On the table near an armchair, which she hardly ever leaves these days, is a photograph of a young man; next to it, a small vase of flowers. 'That's my son, my little boy . . . he's gone from this world now . . .' she always says. A neighbour brings in her coal and runs a few errands for her. Another woman looks in from time to time. And that's about the extent of her contact with the outside world.

After every visit, just as I am about to leave, she says, 'You will come back and see me again, won't you Father?'

I always hesitate, then I say yes.

How does one handle this place where practically every house has old people in it living alone, often abandoned? I don't want to be a social worker, visiting the sick and the aged. I'm not made for that sort of thing! I know all the arguments: old people have to be organised and taught to take care of themselves and each other, local care-for-the-elderly groups should be formed; the existing agencies should be supported, so should home care, centres for the aged; people, society, the Church, must be made to face their responsibilities and help the aged to live and die in dignity; we must do this, we must do that . . . Yes, yes, I know, I agree. But it still doesn't change the fact that this afternoon, Mrs X. asked me to go and see her again and I said yes, because all the social security agencies in the world can never replace a friendly gesture.

The problem is, where do you draw the line? You can only do so much.

147

Man's arrogance never ceases to amaze me. He has become so big and powerful, so much in control of so much of the universe . . . yet he doesn't see that there are still things he hasn't yet discovered and that his science is only in its infancy.

He has penetrated the subconscious enough to gain great

knowledge and discover the source of man.

He is very advanced in his study of man in society and within its economic and political structures and knows what he should know; he can analyse all society and all structures and measure their value and influence.

Finally when those who study the universe, man and society have studied and understood everything, they will still be faced with the unknown, the incomprehensible — the monumental mystery of the 'senses' which, for all their science and knowledge, they will never fathom.

Yes, I'm amazed that man should still be so arrogant because it seems to me that the more knowledge and power he acquires, the more he should be aware of his own ignorance and weakness.

148

I wrote earlier (see No. 74) that people are beginning to realise that materialism is not the key to happiness. Many young people are groping in the dark for new ways, new places. When they meet someone who seems to know what they need, or are looking for, they converge on him; they need such people to guide them, people with insight and wisdom, 'seers' who can look beyond the visible.

I like little Bernadette because as she looked in that gap in the rock, she could SEE . . . beyond. People came to her in great numbers from everywhere, kneeling motionless for hours, oblivious of the police and their attempts to get people moving. Threats of arrest fell on deaf ears as people waited to SEE what Bernadette could see. But they couldn't; so they looked at her and saw that she *could* see. I must be able to see, and when others look at me, they must be able to see that I can see.

Very soon we shall need priests committed to the fight to make this world a better one, but we shall also need priests who contemplate — 'seers', men of 'insight'. For what is the use of building a better world if we don't know why, or for what or whom?

149

I'm travelling by train. I like writing in trains because I feel free and peaceful. There are no appointments to keep, no telephones ringing, no letters to answer or files to be read. On trains I can escape that uneasy feeling that I should be doing something useful, that I'm shortchanging the people who have a right to my time. Just to sit at my desk and write is a luxury to me.

It's a lovely day. The fields and burgeoning trees are bathed in sunlight. Nature is coming to life again as the train hurtles past it. I am seized by a wild desire to stop, freeze the scene and look at it — to stand motionless before nature and contemplate it. And beyond nature, man, humanity, history, life, love, my love and my source, 'the' source. But the train keeps moving, fast, faster, towards the city, leaving fields and trees, houses and roads behind; ships that pass in the night; such a rapid passage that there's no time to look, to see. And I'm left with an unquenched thirst.

I've spent my life rushing around, but I've also felt a deep need to stop, to sit down. Oh, to be able to pause, look and see! And to see within, beyond the façade. To rejoin beauty and life. To commune.

Sometimes I summon back images of landscapes I've seen and in my imagination, I find myself before them, rubbing the eyes of my soul and heart like a man waking up and wondering whether it was all a dream. But none of it is a dream — I've seen some wonderful things.

Driving into Moscow I saw the red stars shining in the black night of the city, and St Basil on guard before the Kremlin.

I've seen that white river, the Saint Lawrence, stretching endlessly into the Canadian landscape, carrying along ice and snow.

I've flown over the peaks of the Andes and seen them so close that I've been afraid they would tear into the belly of the plane.

I've seen Rio's bay, the Copacabana, the moon shining over the sea at night in Salvador de Bahia.

I've seen the syrup drip from the maple trees in the forests of Canada.

I've seen wild animals roaming the plains of Zimbabwe.

I've seen the Victoria Falls and the island of monkeys.

I've seen Mount Fujiyama, Japanese gardens, cherry trees in bloom, temples and buddhas.

I've seen glaciers in the North Pole; immense sugar plantations in Cuba; coffee plantations in Brazil; the Argentinian pampas. I've seen so much.

No, that's not quite true. I haven't really *seen* anything. I've been too busy being jolted around in jeeps on bumpy roads, hot and thirsty, wishing the trip would end. In planes, trains and buses, I would work on my speeches. During the visits themselves, I'd be lucky to get an hour's sightseeing; it was usually a matter of 'Hurry up, we've got to be at wherever in forty minutes.' People, questions, problems constantly surrounded me, and when it was all over, I carried the weight of it all as well as the meeting and suffering and more problems.

But subconsciously, I myself didn't allow for any 'distraction'. I told myself I was on a mission not a vacation — or even a study trip. I would think of my colleagues back home working in their parishes. Going further back into the past, enriched by an unforgettable experience encompassing four years, I would think of all the workers, glancing at their watches, wishing for an end to their long day. I did not wish — and I still don't wish it — especially because I'm a priest, to enjoy myself while others toiled and suffered.

The train continues on its way. It seems to be going faster and faster. The countryside rushes by. Life rushes by. Life is rushing on and I'm not living it. Neither are the people around me. They've all climbed aboard the same train, the one that runs too fast. We're all mad!

Pull the alarm. Stop the train and let the people off. Let them look around them, let them contemplate, let them live.

How do we get to the point of looking but not seeing, touching but not feeling, hearing but not listening, ageing but not living?

We're all going to have to learn how to live all over again.

150

It seems God has spoken. Is it possible?

'Yes, he's spoken. God has spoken to all men.'

'But who can understand God's language?'

'All men, because he spoke to them in their own words, in their own history.'

'Marvellous. Now tell me quickly how I can nourish myself with this Word.'

'Nothing simpler. Let me explain:

'First of all you need a method. Several methods to be precise. Luckily we have many tools of 'scientific' analysis at our disposal to help us avoid all possibility of error. First, you have the 'historico-critical method' by which you can discover the cultural context in which a text was written. Nothing simpler with which to reconstruct this universe. You, of course, start with a literary and textual analysis — this is indispensable — and, aided by archeology, sociology, economics, politics, history and pre-history (because you must also know the conditions under which the text was written), you can find out what the author was trying to say, who he said it to, in what milieu and in what circumstances he said it. At the same time, you need a little biblical theology so as not to stray from the unity of the Word, at once discovering the richness, the grand designs and the personal theology of the author. In a general fashion, of course, you now know much more than your parents ever knew, those poor ignorant people who thought it all stopped at 'exegesis'. You, naturally, have graduated to 'hermeneutics', interpreting old truths for modern use.

'Let's be honest, though. If you only use one method, you're bound to make mistakes. Fortunately for you, there are scholars who've advanced other marvellous methods of analysis — structural analysis, for instance, which allows you to step from the diachronic study of language to a synchronic one — that is to say, in simpler terms, you are now in the field of semiotics (and don't ever call it 'semiology', it's passé). Materialist analysis will help you see that the text was written within the socio-economic structures of the time; so all you need do is reconstruct these structures and contexts of the time to understand the text and its author.

'Before I continue, I would like to counsel you (just to be on the safe side) to wait until scholars come up with more methods of analysis — you won't have long to wait; they're always coming up with something or other. Scholars are always correcting the gross errors of their predecessors. One musn't rush things; the stakes here are too high.

'If, however, you find you're still impatient to know what God has said, you can throw all caution and scholarship to the wind and start by reading the text itself. (You've only studied it so far; you've never actually *read* it.) You'll find it quite an adventure. This time it's just you and the text. And your understanding of it will be entirely subjective; you may identify with people, places and things it contains. In fact, you'll be conducting a dialogue with yourself. You'll hear your own words (more comfortable than hearing God's Word), you'll make your own interpretations and you'll see all your beliefs and ideologies wonderfully confirmed. If you're part of a movement, don't be afraid — your word will guide you and the Word of God will remain in line with the movement, even if the Word's meaning changes . . . I mean, don't worry about it, it's not serious. Any psycho-analyst's handbook will help you out there! But then again you might hang on until a revised version of it comes out; you never know what discoveries they may come up with! After the Lacanian, the Freudian for sure (classical and neo-classical), then the Jungian, and who knows what else. Have yourself analysed, as needed. All you need are a few years to spare. Your interpretation will change through the different stages of analysis but then all you'll have to do is synthesise the different interpretations.

'It's really all very simple. Read a dozen good books, attend a two-week course or something, a few lectures and seminars, and you're all set. The best thing, of course, would be to be able to take a couple of years off and go and study the whole thing in depth. But this sort of thing costs money and not all of us can afford it. (Between you and me, people just don't know how to make sacrifices any more!)'

'Thank you so much for all this advice and information, but isn't there a quicker way?'

'Certainly, but you'll have to take a plane.'

'A plane?'

'Yes, to Africa or South America, to north-eastern Brazil for instance. There, at Sertao, I advise you to go and see the poverty-stricken peasants, especially the ones who've never seen the inside of a classroom but have learned to read anyway so that they can read the Bible. They'll explain God's Word to you.'

'Do they know everything?'

'Yes, they've learned it all.'

'Who was their teacher?'

'A great spirit. Over there they call him the Holy Spirit.'

'Couldn't you invite this Holy Spirit person to come and give us a lecture or two?'

'Impossible. He lives much too far away. The cost would be prohibitive!'

(I scribbled the above during a lecture given by a so-called scholar. He bored me. I confess very humbly that I should have made more of an effort to listen to him; I also confess that I can be quite a severe judge. But what I'm criticising here is not the method but its *abuse*. My great fear is that genuine understanding of the Scriptures will be swallowed up and disappear under the scientific scalpel. True understanding of the Scriptures does not come from mere intellectual study.)

151

Freedom without love is fear and constraint, which can ultimately lead to war. Because where freedom is established without love, force must be employed to maintain it.

152

Death begins the day we are born. Living is a series of deaths and births. Those who don't accept death refuse life. Psychologists know this, and they teach people how best to live the stages in between the first birth and the last death, or, to put it another way, the various 'deaths' of our existence: childhood must die for adolescence to be born, adolescence must give way to adulthood. And when old age is upon us, we must prepare for the mysterious journey which does not lead to *another* life but to the *other* life.

Jesus said that he who clings to his life loses it; he who accepts losing it, finds it.

153

Some people rightly point out that these days we're concerned more with rights than duties. It's a serious matter; but the question of rights has two sides to it — right on the one, duty on the other. *One cannot exist without the other.*

To talk to young people only of gaining and defending their rights is to do them a great disservice and introduce them to constant dissatisfaction. And, what's worse, it is to burden them with the impossible task of having to build a world of peace and justice.

154

Before giving the floor to the 'thinkers' at meetings, let's give it to the 'doers'.

Yes . . . but the problem is they're not present — they're out working.

155

I arranged to meet her at the railway station. She was a journalist and had telephoned me to ask for an interview just as I was about to leave, so I asked her to meet me at the train. We could talk there.

How was I going to recognise her though? I realised only after I hung up that I didn't know what she looked like. There was no problem however — somehow I recognised her. There are all sorts of signs one picks up.

I thought about that on the train. *Lord, is it because I don't know you well enough through the Gospel that, too often, I fail to see you in daily life?* Yet you're there, signalling to me in the middle of the crowds, at the railway station and everywhere else. Meeting you in the Scriptures, or meeting you in the streets — one is futile without the other. Together they are everything. I believe this with all my strength, but I don't practise it enough. Yet I know, from experience, that every time I stray a little from the Gospel (whether on my own or with one of the groups I work with), I experience a drought, and end up with a meagre harvest.

Lord, I still use the Gospel in my apostolic duties. I must come to you freely. I must look at you, contemplate you, discover, if I can, your ways of acting and being. I must know this from within, your thoughts, your joys, your anguish. To love. To commune. And having thus become more intimate with you, I can follow in your steps and get to know you again. (Thank you, Madam Journalist! You did well to phone me.)

156

I'm very sensitive to noise. Noise is the curse of the modern world, another form of pollution. We're going to need an awful lot of work to clean it up and I, for one, don't know how we're going to manage it.

157

We have to learn how to breathe, walk, feel, listen, express ourselves, and so on, all over again. There are many 'therapies' around to help us.

I don't know if we fully realise how distressing this problem is. Educated people, their heads stuffed with science and knowledge, have to go back to kindergarten — they've forgotten their very first, basic lessons.

I've met some of these people. Intensely serious, learning all over again how to talk, sing, shout, gesticulate. A therapist had them doing 'exercises' — games we played as children. I saw them once in the country, doing these exercises in the middle of a field. The farm hands watched them, amused. The kids burst out laughing. They didn't have to pay someone to teach them how to express themselves.

158

Forget about sharing 'ideas', especially 'beautiful ideas', on the Gospel. Concentrate rather on sharing a life transformed by the Gospel.

159

Many people aren't at ease with the Old Testament. It seems to me they've forgotten that Jesus came and proclaimed: 'They told you this, but I tell you . . .'

There are Christians and even whole nations who have the mentality of the Old Testament. Perhaps it's because we haven't 'evangelised' them enough.

160

What a gap there is between dreams and reality! At one time, I wanted to be poor among the poorest, forgoing all comfort, all life's little pleasures. Some of the ideas and attitudes I used to have would make anyone smile to-day.

I gradually came to believe, however, that some things weren't that important, that one was human after all and, in short, that a bit of happiness wasn't a bad thing.

Still I don't think I'm one hundred per cent convinced. The fact remains that I am a disciple of the man who died naked on the cross, crying out in his loneliness.

I know I tell others that it's not a question of choosing a cross — those imposed on us are heavy enough without having to go looking for more — but I'm also aware that it's very easy to look for the easier way, one where hopefully crosses are absent.

161

I don't like discussing 'ideas'. I don't see the point, especially when it's just an exercise in persuading oneself that one is right. At best, one can play with ideas; I don't believe you can discuss them and end up with cut-and-dried conclusions. Intelligent people know this.

I do admire people who can talk about everything; sometimes I envy them that ability.

I don't have the time to go looking for ideas in books and libraries. Fortunately, however, I do have my own source — life. All I have to do is look and listen. But my ideas aren't glamorous; they're ordinary, everyday ones. Perhaps they're more solid and realistic, and therefore more useful.

162

'God called him home.' I hate this so-called act of faith. It's not God who decides people's death. He is always beside them through this mysterious and painful mutation, just as he is with the seed buried in the soil, about to germinate.

163

It's not a matter of applying the Gospel to your life, or inserting it in there somewhere.

It's a matter of taking nourishment from the Gospel and gradually acquiring a Gospel mentality, a Gospel reaction.

164

I'm happy to have met X. I met him through a mutual friend and had a long conversation with him. He told me where he worked — what a dump! I know his company by reputation. It's a place where they squeeze their employees dry to get 'maximum production'. How many people have had their lives shortened there, I hate to think. I listened to him avidly. Perhaps it was because I was disposed to being sympathetic, or because I had prayed at length that very morning, or even because these workers X was talking about and their life of struggle touched me profoundly, to the depths of my being, there where the life of others meets mine. It's at that point that I *know* lives meet and mingle in some mysterious fashion. And I find myself engrossed in a new lifestyle, as I am this evening. Will I be able to see it through, nourish it, help it grow in the light of your love? Already it is stirring in me and hurting me. Birth is always painful.

I have before me a map of Le Havre showing the most important work centres. I've noted the presence of activists (JOC members); I've even prayed before this map. I feel I have to, but I don't do it enough. It's never easy to stop and 'waste' time before God and life, when life calls. But despite my lack of faithfulness, I think I'm doing better these days.

Thanks to the young men and women of the JOC movement and their fellow militants, I am more involved in the workers' struggle and in their lives. I'm no longer just a spectator looking in, guessing, imagining. I am with them. They talk to me and tell me about their lives, their struggles, their triumphs and failures. I listen. I welcome.

Lord, I know very well that their lives can run off me like water off a duck's back. I know that it can all disappear from my life without a trace, and leave me only with something to talk about now and then. On the other hand, their lives can penetrate my soul — as this morning — and become a part of me. If you are there in the depths of my soul (because I have been open enough to you), I really think I could quietly offer you my own life, heavy with other lives and their suffering, and with my hand in yours, together, we'll offer everything to the Father.

At the end of the long night, He will return this life to us, forever renewed. Then will I be able to talk of meetings and reunions.

165

Mr X. came to see me a few days ago about his eldest daughter's problems. Then he wanted me to meet her. This sort of demand always annoys me. Why do parents take us for magicians who can repair years of damage in their children's upbringing with one wave of a magic wand?

I know and like Mr X. well. He's an honest, hard-working man. Both he and his wife kill themselves working. If you want security, you have to work hard, he told me. And work hard they do; their business has grown and prospered. He also added: 'We're working for our kids. I hope when they're older they'll realise what we've done for them.'

I talked to the daughter. Not only has she problems, but they're much more serious than her father knows. After we had talked I asked her why she hadn't discussed all this with her parents.

'I don't know my parents! We don't talk much, they're always working.'

'But they're doing it for you.'

'So what? It's not what I need!'

It would be very easy to throw stones at these unhappy

parents who would be genuinely puzzled and upset if they knew what was going on. They're not the only guilty ones. It's never the fault of just one thing, it's a combination of many. If small businessmen didn't have to work so hard to get anywhere, they would have more time to spend with their children. On the other hand, we still have a choice. What does success mean to us? What happiness are we striving for? We must make the choice.

It's so much easier to love when you're poor.

166

Praying is a lot less complicated than we think. To begin with, it's talking to God who is in our lives and the lives of our brothers. A young person may say: 'I talk to him, but he never answers.'

I answer: 'That's wrong. He's the one who talks to you first (through the prophets and his Son). Then there's his Gospel. God speaks to you through the mouths of men. Answer him. It's only polite.'

He says: 'And if I don't understand something, can I come to you?'

I answer: 'Not so fast. Tell him you don't understand what he's saying. And continue reading. He'll explain a little further on.'

167

In a train that's taking me to Tokyo after a day in the south of Japan, we pass Hiroshima.

It's been five or six years since I was in Nagasaki delivering a lecture. There I visited the atomic bomb museum. Three images from the place have stayed with me, firmly planted in my memory.

Opposite a huge staircase, a wall is covered with all manner of clocks, all hideously mutilated. They all stopped at the same time — suspended time.

In the main hall there is another wall on which, as if on a giant screen, the radiation blast of the bomb projected the silhouette of a group of men who must have been passing by or pausing in conversation. These tragic shadows are all that remains of them.

Finally, in a glass case, a hand still holding a bottle. It was dinner time; someone was about to drink from the bottle. Now the hand and the bottle are forever mangled and fused together.

How could I ever forget!

In the evenings, after my lectures, I would go and spend some time by myself in the Garden of Peace, a beautiful, green, flowering park on the very spot where the bomb fell. I tried to pray but the thought that today's living flourish on yesterday's dead made me angry. We are such creatures of habit. How soon we forget. Life goes on.

Today, as the train goes by Hiroshima, that thought comes back to haunt me. The town has grown; it's now a city of over a million inhabitants. The whole world chipped in to rebuild it out of a need for forgiveness, a need to replaster our cracked consciences and paint them white. Now it's done. We've done our duty. And we are free, in peace, to find good reasons to manufacture more bombs and create more Hiroshimas.

Oh my God, my Lord, suffering on your enormous cross, planted there in Hiroshima, once more you are silent. Oh *why?*

Dark clouds of shame over Hiroshima
Which saw in one-tenth of a second
Two hundred thousand stripped of their life.
Grimy factory spitting out the smoke of the usurpers'
                                                                    handywork.
Black night of my heart,
Active volcano simmering with muffled revolt,
Dark clouds of Hiroshima.

Where are the dead?
I look but I can't see them,
I look but I can't hear them.
I hear the noises of the city,
I hear footsteps, voices, laughter,
A million lives walking over their ashes.
Where are the dead?
Wake up! Speak!
Come tell us of the scorching heat,

105

the smell of sulphur,
   the taste of ashes.
Come back, finish what you were saying,
   drink from the bottle,
   embrace your loved one.
Interrupted life, snuffed-out people
Dust, shadows, night, nothingness.
Silence of the dead
Silence of God

Why are the dead silent? I want to hear their voices!
   Shout! Scream! Tell us it's unjust.
   Tell us we're all mad!
'They will not be convinced even if someone should rise
                         from the dead' (Luke 16:31).

Soil of Hiroshima, keep your dead.
But you, my Lord God,
Fearsome, silent God, crucified on the cross,
Speak, shout, wake us!
Tell us we must love!
'At various times in the past and in various different ways,
God spoke to our ancestors through the prophets but in
our own time, the last days, he has spoken to us through
                  his son . . .' (Hebrews 1:1 and 2).
So be it.
Jesus, won't you speak either?
'But he was silent and made no answer at all' (Mark 14:61).

The train rolls on, and on.
Around me, people laugh, and laugh . . .
My heart is sick, I just want to sleep . . .
I close my eyes
'So you had not the strength to keep awake with me one
                  hour?' (Matthew 26:40).

Night falls in Hiroshima.

168

While transcribing the above notes and poem, I thought of
my first journey to Japan, that first feeling of revolt that I

felt at Hiroshima, and the Lord's answer through a young girl's sensitive gesture.

I had just finished lecturing in Tokyo. Among the people who had attended and who stayed behind to ask me questions, or even wanted my autograph, a young girl came up to me. 'I live in Hiroshima,' she said. 'I'm going back tonight. I came specially to thank you for your books; my friends thank you too.' With that she handed me a prettily wrapped package. I opened it. Inside was a beautiful Japanese painting. 'I did it myself,' she said. The characters painted on the canvas read, in Japanese, 'Light and Life'. I thanked her, but it wasn't enough. She disappeared quickly into the crowd. I don't know her name or her address. I can't even write to her. Should she ever read these lines, I want her to know that *God hasn't stopped talking*. It's just that now he's talking through the lives of loving people. Sometimes he speaks through the heart and paint-brush of a Japanese girl. I've only just realised it myself — thanks to her.

169

We should meditate often on the discovery and mastery of atomic energy. This triumph of man is at once *the pride of the Father and the passion of the Son*. Pride of the Father because man grows bigger every day under God's gaze. He becomes what he was meant to be: master of the universe. Passion of the Son, because Jesus, ever in empathy with his brothers, continues to suffer and die, torn apart and atomised by man who grows more and more powerful but less and less loving. Is man growing too fast? Only if love doesn't grow accordingly. Remember: what good is it if man gains the universe if he also loses his soul? We are so guilty if we, as Christians, don't remind the world of this.

170

Once again I was asked what I talk about in my lectures. I replied: Jesus Christ, and at the top of my voice!

It's true. I've always done just that. I still do. Wherever I am. Even when I'm told to be silent.

More than once I've worried my hosts. They would shower

advice on me: above all be discreet, your audience is very mixed, there are important people out there, there are non-Christians out there, talk to them of love, of the meaning of life, of Jesus Christ . . . what do I know?

Whatever the place, or the audience, I always speak of Jesus Christ. I tell myself they know I'm a priest, they've invited me, what do they expect? I've never had any regrets.

But I never try to 'push' Jesus Christ. I say: 'This is what I believe. I'm not forcing you to believe it. I can't give you faith. Faith can't be passed on. I can't transmit it. No one can oblige anyone to believe that he is loved.' No one has objected to my beliefs; people don't usually object to you expressing your beliefs. But they very much object if you try to impose your beliefs on them.

There are times when I'm too detached from Jesus Christ to feel I have any right to speak of him. So I'm tempted to keep quiet (sometimes I'm ashamed that I talk as loudly as I do). But it's just a fleeting temptation. If I waited to be really close to Christ before speaking of him, I'd be waiting forever.

While it doesn't excuse me, what comforts me, Lord, is that you don't mind who your mouthpiece is as long as your message of love gets through to all men. Stay with me, even if I'm not always your best representative.

171

The other evening I spent some time talking to divinity students (this took place in England where I'd been invited to talk to a number of future ministers). I was on form and enjoying myself — at least, at the beginning.

The young wives and fiancées of the divinity students were also present, and one of them was my interpreter — a beautiful young blonde woman who must have made it very easy for her love to offer himself to the ministry.

I spoke to them about young people and their work. I told them how impressed I was to find that their work may have different shapes and forms but that their hopes and aspirations were the same the world over.

Then I tried to decipher the signs that God sends us and talked of how we priests and ministers could respond to them.

We then went on to the sacrosanct issues — which weren't lacking. I noticed a certain atmosphere of hesitation, as if there were some questions they weren't sure they should ask me. What we needed was a volunteer. He introduced himself hesitantly, a little embarrassed: 'You know young people very well,' he began. 'But . . . how can you understand their love affairs, their engagements, marriages . . . you're celibate. . .?' I'd been expecting this one. I put on a solid expression and asked my interpreter what her first name was. Jenny, she said. Who was Jenny's fiancé? He presented himself.

First I congratulated him on his good taste (laughter); then I said I felt very very sorry for him (stunned silence). Poor Jenny, who was obliged to interpret this, didn't know where to look.

'When you become ministers,' I said, 'sooner or later one of your parishioners will come to you and tell you all his family problems. After you've listened to him, you'll say: 'Yes, I know my dear fellow, I can well understand you. Sometimes even Jenny and I . . .' He won't let you finish. 'No, you don't understand, you couldn't possibly — you and Jenny, it's not the same thing; a woman like her, it must be wonderful. If you were in my shoes, you'd see, my wife is . . .' and so on and so forth. That's why, my friend, I feel very sorry for you. Because if you want to be a good minister to your parishioners, you're condemned to marry their wives one after another. Jenny's not going to like it.'

The tension eased. Everyone laughed. I gave another example: 'Before coming here, I chatted with some of you. I asked you if, along with your academic education, you had received a pastoral one. You said yes, and one of you told me he visited prisons, that he was very involved in prison work and understood the prisoners' problems well. But how can this be so? Has he experienced the same problems? Has he been in prison?'

There I was, a celibate — no one doubted that — who'd written a girl's diary (*The Journal of Anne-Marie*). So many adolescents had written to say how well it expressed their feelings, happiness, suffering, questions. How could you know so perfectly how we feel, they asked. Because I had simply tried to listen to them with the eyes and ears of my heart.

There are many ways of knowing the people around us, whether we experience the same things or whether we're 'empty' enough to be able to receive the experiences of others to the point of making them our own. The only obstacle is the weakness of our love. Ministers or priests, we must join our lives to the lives of others. This is Christ's way; he pushed it to perfection, to the point where all people were united in one body, each of us a part of it.

The real value of our ministry will be measured against our capacity for communion.

172

Demanding responsibility and actually achieving it are worlds apart. In between lies an area in which one must first become transformed.

173

I've just seen J. He told me he didn't want a 'spiritual advisor', but he's looking for a guru.

Well, we all need new words now and then; we use words so mercilessly that we wear them out in no time at all.

174

I wonder if people in general aren't essentially a sad lot! They're always looking for amusement, distraction — even more so these days. When they're working, they're planning their leisure time — during the day, evenings; during the week, the week-end; during the year, annual vacations. Is it because they haven't found their hidden treasure, that is, the meaning of life?

Life is a treasure hunt.

Those in love have found their treasure. They're happy even if times are hard. They know what they're struggling for, and for whom — their husbands, their wives (their treasure) and their children (their little treasures). But a husband, a wife and children don't exhaust their capacity for happiness. There still remain traces of sadness in their hearts.

Does man always have the taste of paradise lost in his

mouth? Is he searching for THE treasure?

The one who finds the treasure buried in a field, the Gospel tells us, reburies it. In his happiness he sells all his goods and buys the field (see Matthew 13:44).

I must help men find their treasure; I must hunt with them in the field of their lives and encourage them to dig. But once they find it, they'll have to sell a lot of their belongings — will I have the courage to make sure they do?

175

I don't like holidays. I prefer to work. I'm not being a hero; it's just that I get bored when I'm not working. And I'm happy to have a quiet holiday to work in. Today, however, I've had the odd feeling that I've been waiting for someone. Every time the doorbell rings, I jump up thinking that perhaps it's for me. Every time the telephone rings, I think it's for me. It never is. There's no one here, I tell callers. No one?

I mean no one except myself. I'm here, but I'm not supposed to be. I realise I've been waiting all day for a little company, some human warmth, someone, anyone, to justify my reason for being here — and to allow me to give of myself.

No one calls.

I must give myself in silence, in solitude, without being asked, without anyone to smile and say, 'Thanks. I'm so glad you were in.'

I'm not in for anyone.

I begin thinking about solitude. Loneliness. All the old people who wait for me, who've been waiting for weeks, months, years. And no one comes. No one will come. They're not supposed to be in for anyone either. Oh, they were in when they were useful, when they could do something for you, when they could meet your demands. Now it's all over. They've nothing left to give, or so we think. It's their turn to receive. But those who received yesterday have no time to give today. They're busy elsewhere. Maybe they're busy giving. But also taking, wherever there's still something left to take.

I'm no longer alone. I'm with all the lonely people. Somehow we're all united, together in this night of a million solitudes.

If they only knew that I was there with them, taking on their pain, carrying it with them, giving it some meaning.

Shared suffering is easier to bear. I want you to know that even suffering can be constructive.

176

I had sensed that he wanted to talk to me, but he was hesitant. I could understand him. Finally, he came, sat down, his shoulders hunched. A moment's silence, and he shook himself like a man unable to carry his crippling burden any longer. 'I'm a homosexual,' he said very quickly. I looked at him quietly, in a friendly way, and said firmly. 'No.'

'But I should know! Why, only the other day . . .'

'NO. You're not a homosexual. You're Raoul.'

Raoul. That's who he was. A man of great personal qualities (he was so surprised when I pointed out a few of them just by looking at him); a man who does wonderful things with his life (I'd heard about some of them); a man who is especially loved by God; a man with homosexual tendencies who, at times, practised them. Whatever the pain his homosexuality caused him, nothing could ever take away the fact that *he was Raoul, beloved of God.* This was the wonderful reality. The rest was relatively unimportant.

We talked for a long time. Gradually he relaxed. I hardly dared look at him because I was afraid of embarrassing him. I didn't want him to think that I was 'examining' him. When our eyes finally met, we could only smile at each other, and I was as happy as he was because I felt he understood my smile was genuine.

I wasn't able to solve his dilemma, but I helped him rediscover himself — a rich human being, dignified and kind, *facing* his problems without fear. Until then he had been rejecting himself, believing that God and other people had rejected him. But now I could help him look for ways of dealing with his suffering.

What holds true for all our infirmities holds equally true for our sins. We identify ourselves — or are identified — with our sins. And we hate ourselves — and are hated — along with our sins. This is wrong. Whatever the enormity of our sin, *we must never lose our self-respect*, because we are always loved and respected. God suffered not because of us, but because of our sins. So, for goodness sake, if we throw out our sins, let us not throw ourselves out with them. Our Father waits for us.

177

When men are prepared to die for their ideals but not to kill for them, only then will they be able to say that they've laid the foundations for peace. But humanity is nowhere near that. There's a lot more to be learned on the subject of loving.

178

We want to teach the young how to live their lives before teaching them what their lives are for. They're more logical than us — before they learn how to live, they want to know why they're living.

179

We wanted to draw up a timetable of masses, so we consulted our parishioners. I warned them beforehand that there would be a few who wouldn't get the times they wanted — it would be a majority decision. I didn't want them to say, 'They consult us but don't give us what we want.'

I couldn't have been more right. One of them got very angry indeed. I tried, unsuccessfully, to calm him down. Most people believe in democracy. Unfortunately for many, democracy means 'Ask me what I think . . . then DO IT.'

180

He's just left, and I'll probably never see him again. He doesn't live in Le Havre (my home). A friend of mine, who thought I might be able to help him, sent him to me. For two hours I tried to put myself entirely at his disposal, and he was happy enough when he left. So was I, but I couldn't help feeling a pang of sadness. I felt I was just a temporary refuge, a stop-over point, and it hurt. Even if you accept being this kind of thing, it's still very very difficult sometimes. All the same, my door will always be open.

Transient friend, come in. If you're hungry, sit down, the table is set. I won't keep you long! Put down your load and eat. Rest yourself.

You're leaving? Does your burden feel lighter? Yes, it's because you're stronger. My bread is nourishing, my God helps me knead it, then he bakes it in the fire of his love: the Eucharist, the provision for your journey.

By eating with me, you drew nourishment from him.

Continue on your way; we will always be with you, quietly, in mysterious ways, carrying your load.

But if you want to, leave the heavier loads behind if you don't need them. We'll take care of them.

181

If you cut a tree at its roots, you condemn it to death.
If you dry up the source, you eliminate the river.
If you cut yourself off from Christ, you die.
By wanting to eliminate God from their lives, people take
on the responsibility of humanity's suicide.

182

I was called to the bedside of a dying man. A neighbour came to fetch me. She seemed a bit uneasy, but there wasn't time to ask her why. I just wanted to get to the man in time.

He died yesterday. Yet another person who shouldn't have been frightened to die.

I prayed and tried to get his widow to pray too, but I must admit I was a bit distracted. I looked around the tiny room. The bed took up most of the space; the dead man was lying in it. There was a heater, a sink, a cupboard, a side-board and a couple of chairs. And a tiny cluttered-up table. She saw me looking around and guessed what was going through my mind. 'This is all the space we have, Father. I had to sleep in the same bed as Hector last night.' She gestured towards the bed. She had slept in the same bed as her dead husband.

I didn't know what to say. I didn't know what to do. I was helpless before the helpless. I tried to leave.

But I couldn't. They came to take the dead man away. There was hardly any room to get the coffin in.

The undertakers worked quickly. I remarked sarcastically that I hoped they weren't expecting a large tip. And yet, the woman wouldn't let them leave empty-handed. 'Will you have a drink, gentlemen? You too Father.' I couldn't refuse. She picked up four glasses and a bottle of red wine, and looked for somewhere to set them down. I knew instantly what she was going to do. She lifted the cloth from the coffin and set the glasses down on it. Then she poured the wine and we drank.

I thought, well, tomorrow the poor man will finally lie alone in his own patch of earth, even if he did have to wait one day after his death. (This happened when I was new to the parish. But in my second parish, in the same area, I found similar conditions of hardship. Most people don't even know they exist. They don't see it, so they say it doesn't exist, at least not any more. And some are quite sincere. No wonder they're surprised when people riot.)

183

They thought to please me by giving me something they liked. I was, of course, touched by their gesture, but not by their gift (I don't like it at all).

It's difficult to love totally and absolutely — that is, wanting only the happiness of others — theirs, not ours projected on others as a means of realising our own desires. This is only pleasing ourselves through others.

184

When a friend told me that Stanny was dying of cancer in a suburban Paris hospital, I went to him immediately. (Stanny, a character in *Danny's Diary*, is a real person. He came to France as a refugee from Yugoslavia, and was involved in the Catholic Youth Society in Le Havre. Talented and hardworking, he was a newly qualified officer of the Merchant Marine when he fell ill.)

He was in a private room listening to music. His young nurse had lent him a record player and some records. He said she'd given him much more – complete and unreserved affection, even though it couldn't go anywhere. He was lucid; he accepted his fate, yet couldn't understand the meaning of this futile, stupid, dreadful end. 'What good is life if you can't give it,' I said, trying to help him. 'No one owns it, it's a gift, not to keep but to pass on. Every day people pass on their lives, some give it daily, others give it completely all at once. I don't know which is easier. It's impossible to know. The important thing is not the circumstances in which we give up our life, but the strength of the love we give it with.'

In the meantime the nurse had come in to put him on a drip. When she left, I continued: 'Stanny, look at the pin-prick in your arm. It's tiny, yet it allows the serum that keeps you going to penetrate into your body. You're tiny too in this immense world, a speck in the huge body of humanity, but you're *free*. Freedom is scary – you're free not to cling to your life helplessly but to give it in love like Jesus Christ. This way you're adding extra love to a world that needs it.'

He said: 'I know I'm lucky to be able to offer my life voluntarily, but I still haven't the strength to thank God for it. Pray so that I'll be able to!' They were his last words to me.

When I came back up from Le Havre eight days later to see him, he was dead. I kept thinking of what I'd told him. In my notebook I scribbled the following: 'Stanny dies alone in hospital. Alone, anonymous, in silence. It doesn't make sense. There are people who give their lives to a cause, in a public blaze of glory. It is witnessed, known, it serves a purpose: to save other lives, to fight injustice, against an enemy. But Stanny? And all the Stannys of the world who don't even have someone to write about them in a notebook, to read and remember? What purpose does such a death serve – giving up life freely, without being asked for it? What's the use of being a part of humanity then? What use is it if there isn't a lifeline extending throughout this humanity? What good is a life coming from nowhere and going nowhere? What good is a life that isn't made of *love*? And if there's nothing at all, then what is the purpose of life and death?'

185

People today no longer want to make lifelong commitments. This is a serious failure. An adult is someone who can put a lot of thought into what he's doing, with or without outside help, and who is capable of making a definitive choice — whether it is on an occupation or another person. Faithfulness is then his ability to stick with his choice, the will to fight for it, and turn any obstacles into positive elements on his chosen path.

Unfaithfulness is a disease afflicting both the individual and society. Society throws the individual into new experiences which are never brought to any conclusion. Unfaithfulness is to be put off by any obstacles; weakness is man's downfall. Constantly uprooted, he can never reach maturity and bear fruit.

Fidelity within marriage is the most profound of all because the root it takes in the love of each spouse cannot be pulled up. A married couple may grow apart but they can no longer 'unmarry'.

186

Montreal. In a couple of days Abbé Pierre and I will be in Lima. Here in Montreal we've just dined in a magnificent restaurant as guests of some people. People think they have to spend a fortune to please those they respect or love. It's madness, but that's the way it is.

I couldn't eat. I kept thinking of the Latin American tour ahead, and all the poverty we would be seeing. I stole a glance at Abbé Pierre. Was he going to say anything? He was looking a bit tense and he wasn't eating either. He wasn't even pretending to. I could see a storm brewing. And sure enough, it erupted. He began by asking our hosts' forgiveness for what he was about to say and, with some force, indeed violence, he told these good people that they wouldn't be able to make laws and find ways to free the world from its misery unless they consented to experience something of that misery. Otherwise their good will and devotion counted for nothing; it was all a sad illusion and just props to ease their conscience. When he stopped, he was shaking with an anger too long under control . . . and they applauded! For about an hour I listened to the person seated next to me talk about his worries. He was a member of parliament heading a commission to find ways of disposing of surplus grain. I asked, with false naiveté, why didn't they just give it to underdeveloped countries? He explained carefully that they had to distribute donations through a system of quotas, otherwise the shares would drop.

187

Latin America overwhelms me, body and soul. Seduction, love, revolt. At the moment I'm revolted.

Yesterday Montreal. Today Lima. I can't sleep before I write down the frightening contrast between the two.

We landed late in the morning, and by early afternoon we were visiting the Emmaus community in the desert. About a year ago, some people installed themselves on the mountain of garbage (which is why the community is called El Monte) where the city's garbage collectors dumped the city's refuse. They wanted to live among the destitute, who live there just so that they can have first shot at the garbage — for bones, paper, rags . . . and food. The children fight off pigs which are let loose there by their rich owners to feed on the refuse. The community's presence there soon became an embarrassment and, in no time, journalists, TV and radio broadcasters rushed to the scene, followed by curious onlookers. It was written about, talked about, shouted about; an intolerable situation, something must be done, and so on. The Peruvian government was embarrassed into seeking a solution, and decided to award a large piece of land to Emmaus, about thirty or forty kilometres from Lima — in the desert. No roads. No water. No electricity. Just a load of sand. The 'garbage dwellers' hesitated at first, then accepted the offer.

The men — old hobos just out of prison with faces lined by years of misery — and young Swedish volunteers with eyes as blue as the sky and hair the colour of wheat, set up camp. They collected some fifty children from the *barriadas* (shanty towns) — 'wild' children living in packs. They feed them, teach them and give them a little of the happiness they've never known. The garbage dump, however, is still a

118

mine of wealth for them. It's incredible, overwhelming. But the government's problems aren't over yet. The journalists, broadcasters and TV crews return. And the onlookers. More articles, more talk. There's no way this kind of misery can be hidden when it's being fought from within and given a voice, one that can't be silenced.

And I, I'm part of the affluent, surrounded by surplus grain which must be dumped, while there are people living off our *refuse*.

188

(Two or three years later, while visiting French priests in Latin America, I returned to the desert community. It was still there, sitting in the middle of the sands, but by now it was wonderfully developed. I wrote the following that same night.)

Dear Mr President of the Peruvian Republic, I beg your forgiveness. I don't remember what you look like even though I saw you and your wife at the audience you granted Abbé Pierre and me on my first visit. You spoke little; Abbé Pierre did most of the talking. But I just can't remember you. In contrast, I'll never forget the face of the child I met in the desert that same afternoon. I was fascinated by her luminous eyes, too huge for her face, which went from implacable hardness to great softness with amazing speed. We stared at each other and then smiled. She came closer to me, then she stretched out her hand. I opened my arms and she flung herself in them. She put her arms around my neck and squeezed tightly. I thought, 'How strong she is!' Then abruptly she drew back. I loosened my hold, and she looked at me again for a long moment, then kissed me violently on the cheek. When I put her down, she was laughing. She mumbled a few words I couldn't understand and took off.

One of the Swedish volunteers had been watching. She said: 'That's Josette. Three years ago she was found in a trash can. She was only a baby.'

Mr President, it just won't do. You and your people aren't civilised. We are. We don't throw babies in trash cans, unless they're dead. And just to be sure, we sometimes kill them before they've been born, and only doctors and nurses see them as they're disposed of in plastic bags. It's more decent, cleaner, more hygienic. In your country, Mr President, babies thrown into the garbage are in danger of being eaten alive by rats and pigs! (see No. 187).

I am ashamed.

TO THE CHILD OF THE DESERT

Of the landscape of your face, child
I will not remember the black forest of your hair
Or the sand dunes of your chubby cheeks.
I will only remember
The great lakes of your eyes.

Child, tell me your secret
What were you looking for when you put your strong little
                                 arms around my neck
When your lips touched my cheek
Were you hungry, were you thirsty?

Never will I forget
Never do I want to forget
   your parched lips,
   your thirsting eyes.
Come with me child.
I need you.
Don't be afraid — I'm not going to photograph you.
I don't want you frozen on a piece of inanimate paper.
I want you alive, dancing in my heart.
And when I'm weak, wanting only to lie down and sleep,
I will look at you and know your secret.
In you I will see the child Jesus lying in his manger,
And in your eyes
   the man Christ on the cross.
Then I will hear you cry
   twenty centuries old
     I thirst!

Psalm 139 reads:
You had scrutinised my every action,
All were recorded in your book,
My days listed and determined,
Even before the first of them occurred.

Today Abbé Pierre tells me that there are roads being built between Lima and the desert community, as well as water and electricity being installed. The community's land still remains the property of Emmaus. A whole town has mushroomed, with houses, child care centres, studios, schools, with the same people, the same volunteers, the same energy — that 'cry' which many still try in vain to silence.

189

A man has just been talking to me about his emotional anguish following an extramarital affair. He's trying hard to regain his equilibrium, but his family won't allow him to forget his indiscretion. One of them told him just recently: 'The most hateful sin is the sin of the flesh.' The poor man is distraught. He says he loves his wife and children, and I believe him, but that he couldn't resist his desires. He wept in front of me.

I don't *approve* of his behaviour, and I'm sorry for the trouble it's caused, but, listening to him, I really wondered about people who point the finger at only one kind of 'sin of the flesh'. What about tortured flesh in prison camps; hungry and thirsty flesh; flesh enslaved in meagre, underpaid jobs, abandoned sick flesh in hospitals? And we're so full of good intentions and good words! These people have become objects in our hands, more so than the woman in the arms of her lover who desires her as a thirst quenching drink on a hot day.

190

Abbé Pierre is asleep. At least, I hope so. He needs a lot of it. I've been with him a month now on this Latin America tour, watching him, listening to him. Every day he repeats some essential truths: 'The rich have torn out certain pages from the Gospel and thrown them away. With the scavengers, we've found these pages in their trash cans.' He has seized on these words and repeats them tirelessly to one and all — small or large audiences, rich or poor, powerful or ordinary. He begins speaking slowly, as if extracting the words one by one from his tired heart. Some think he's going to collapse.

I know better. His voice picks up, his shoulders straighten and the words emanate stronger, firmer, to the point of sounding violent. Now nothing can stop him. He'll go on until his strength gives out. He'll even need to be helped to stand up or step down from the podium.

In the car taking him back to his room, I watch him — a face covered in an unruly salt-and-pepper beard. Often it takes on a tragic, almost frightening, aura. A steel glint in his eye. Is it anger? Suffering? His face gets tense, his mouth is twisted as if he's in great pain but unable to scream. There has to be a breaking point. Too much tension can be physically damaging. I wait silently. Soon his face relaxes, his jaw loosens up and he sighs, 'Oh my God, oh my God.'

The battle is over for the present.

Then he looks at me, his face glowing gently. 'Do you have everything you need? Is everything alright? You're not too tired I hope...' with infinite gentleness and caring. I couldn't help thinking at that moment of the look on Father Foucauld's face after the Lord had transformed him.

191

Abbé Pierre is speaking. He has the right to speak. This great bourgeois (who'd have believed it?) has opened his heart, even his body, to all the pain and suffering in the world. A successful transplant — which is rare. He has surrendered himself completely, to become fertile ground for all the world. He has become something else, a different man, a new life, a long cry against injustice. For me, Abbé Pierre and Emmaus are a *cry*, a cry that is the clamour of the voices of all men without a voice. This is what prophets are all about.

192

We need politicians although, heaven knows, we have more than enough. We need prophets, but there's a desperate shortage of them. For a prophet is not someone with ideas, shouting them all over the place; a prophet is one whose very life is *word, cry, shout*. A prophet can't help speaking, you'd have to kill him to muzzle him. And even in death, his voice would echo throughout the world.

193

When, tempted by immediate and concrete action, the prophet turns into a politician, he fails in his mission, because if there are no prophets to keep the politicians on their toes, the latter will end up working only for themselves and their party — not for other people.

194

When Christians, or the Church, use the Gospel as a political tool, they abuse and destroy it. The Gospel must remain a *free* call to the world for all time.

195

There are people who help victims of injustice but don't fight injustice itself.

There are others who fight injustice but who fail to help the victims.

The first derive comfort from the fact that they're helping victims; but they're also perpetuating the injustices which create these victims.

The latter may find they're fighting in vain, because their love for mankind isn't powerful enough to purify their struggle. What loving person would say to his wounded brother: 'I'm letting you die. I haven't the time to nurse your wounds because I have to go and fight the one who caused them.'

196

In the struggle against injustice, the Christian suffers a serious handicap which, at least in the short term, can reduce his effectiveness. He doesn't have the right, at any time, to walk over his adversary or destroy him. He doesn't have the right to 'sacrifice' one single person today (let alone a generation) to save a thousand tomorrow.

197

He was a non-violent man, a priest who'd volunteered for work in Latin America. When I saw him again, he said: 'There are times when I want to go out and get myself a machine gun. I hope I never do because I'd be tempted to use it.'

I don't condemn him, I understand him only too well. It's easy to be cool about it all from a distance, reading a few articles and books on under-development and the misery that comes out of it. It's easy to discuss the problems calmly and logically and find ways and means of solving them. But when you're on the spot and have to watch children die of hunger, men being crushed and humiliated daily, all reason and logic go straight out of the window. Anger rises in you like a volcano ready to erupt, with all the pent-up violence of centuries of hunger, torture, slavery. You'd have to be unconscious or a complete monster not to understand.

198

Who are all these ignorant hypocrites who go around preaching against 'violence that solves nothing', 'that causes needless bloodshed', and 'that is unchristian'? Have they given one thought to the thousands and millions who have been dying in the concentration camps of destitution? How many children die daily when they should be living and healthy, not only in Latin America but right here at home. How many will be dead in ten years' time, in a hundred years' time? Before this mountain of dead bodies, I'll also shout my hatred for violence, but I also know (and I can prove it) that all the revolutions and all the wars of liberation in the world haven't created half as many victims. So, all you 'disciples of peace', be quiet. If you must speak, then go and tell all those who are condemned to die to be patient, wise and calm. You go and tell them you're thinking of them, discussing them, crying for them, but that they musn't rebel, oh no, it would only cause the death of many innocents . . .!

199

When I was in north-eastern Brazil I asked what those masks covering children's mouths were. I was told that the children were so hungry that they ate the dirt, which they would dig up looking for roots. The masks were to prevent them from doing this.

200

I have as much violence in me as I have boundless tenderness. The battle of these two emotions often exhausts me. Faced with intolerable injustice (especially in the Third World), my blood boils and I'm pushed to fight. But what army can I join? Then at times my reason whispers calm things to me. And I remain torn in two.

Perhaps, deep in me, these two emotions should unite. Oh Christ, won't you perform this difficult union for me? Won't you then help the fruit of this union to become a *violent love*, as Helder Camara describes it?

Enlighten me, Lord. Tell me what to do. The blood of my brothers cries out to me and I can't sleep.

201

The aircraft is flying at 900 km per hour on the return journey from Latin America, yet it feels completely still. A glass of juice sits before me, perfectly motionless. Everything seems frozen. Yet I've just experienced a spiritual storm such as I've never known. Quick, terrifying, dizzying. In just a few seconds, I felt as if all the obsessive questions and struggles I've had had hit me in one blow. There's so much poverty, injustice, suffering and death, and what am I doing about it? What good am I? Has my life been one big mistake?

All I do is talk, give lectures, address meetings. And I write, telling others what to do, helping them to find the true meaning of life and history, trying to guide them towards Christ — the only sure way, in my opinion, to individual and collective freedom.

Having urged my brothers thus, and having armed them

with tools so that they can fight (have I done it well?), I retreat from the battlefield into my office. Safe, alone in my room, I am still haunted by the ghosts of the oppressed — a terrible image of twisted faces that I can't shake off. I remain alone with my dream of total giving, lost somewhere in the mists and darkness of my weaknesses, perpetually torn between my boundless good will and the crucifying limits of my capabilities.

My imagination, my paralysing doubts and futile, energy-wasting dreams of heroism, wasted tears falling into a sterile earth, all surge within me.

It's so difficult to accept that one is only a very tiny cog in a gigantic wheel, so minuscule as to seem useless. Vertigo, that's what it is. Lost in the eye of the storm. An empty bottomless space. My life. What's a life worth? Millions and millions of lives coming and going since the beginning of time . . . to what end?

Pulling myself together, I looked in my appointment book. I had to attend a meeting that very evening, so I set about preparing for it. The storm had blown over, all was calm again. I thought: After all that, if I can't bring something worth while to this meeting, then I give up.

202

We are stuck between the past and the future. The past is no longer in our hands. Neither is the future since it doesn't exist yet.

The only time we have control over is the present. It is *now*, it exists. It's not heavy to bear, and it's livable by all, on one condition: that we let the past go, and not be impatient for the future.

The present moment passes quickly; before you know it, it's in the past while another present takes its place, as light and narrow and fleeting as the preceding one.

When you live in the past or the future, you lose your present without even living it. Even if you reach the age of ninety, you'll have only really lived twenty or thirty years. And when your Father asks for your life, you won't have much to offer him — just a few years and a lot of lost time.

The only way to 'fill your life' is to live the present fully.

203

I saw you, X., in between smiles; but I only got to know you in between sobs.

204

I don't love you because of Jesus Christ, I love you because you're yourself. But when I love you enough not to demand anything of you, but to give you all, that's because I love you through Jesus.

Only freely given love can truly reach a person and only then does it become touched by God.

205

Very often I find myself on the fringes of happiness. I am not fully happy because I don't always give easily and giving hurts me at times, especially as I'm not free to always be available. If you want to be happy, give, without counting or regrets. Be all-welcoming. Happiness is there for the taking, but you must make room for it.

206

Following the tragic death of a friend of mine, I needed to talk to someone about it. I discovered once again how compelling our need is to talk about such things and not just painful events but happy ones as well. It just bursts inside and can't be contained in the narrow, deep solitude of our being.

I looked for someone who had known my friend well, or even a little, to tell them the terrible news; but, in reality, I was just looking for someone with whom to share the pain. This is our profound need — to call out to another and share the burden. Shared suffering always brings a little relief. Again I told myself: Help others to talk. Listen to them quietly, don't worry about saying the right things or saying anything at all. Just be welcoming, people need your support in carrying their pain.

207

Being welcoming is allowing the other person to invest in you.

208

True freedom doesn't mean being able to do anything you please with your body, heart and soul, when and where you wish, with no restraints or taboos. This sort of freedom only betrays an absence of freedom. It's a form of total alienation; man giving in, on his knees, to all his compulsions. It's going backwards, reverting to his animal condition. An animal lives by its instincts, programmed to fulfil its needs and its growth. But man must master his life and gradually learn how to direct it.

209

Freedom doesn't mean being free for *nothing*! It means being free to *love*. As Abbé Pierre often says: 'If you are free and I'm not sure that you love me, I'm afraid of you. So I do the only thing I know will protect me — I look for a way to make you even more afraid of me.'

210

Seeing the youth club again (in the parish of Sainte-Anne du Havre) reminded me of Joseph when he came to give us a talk. It had been my second or third JOC meeting and the first time I'd met a federal official of the organisation. I was very impressed; Joseph had no notes or books before him, just the Gospel from which he read a passage. I don't remember what passage, but I still remember how I felt. I was moved. God's word was truly reaching me through this man. I was like a child, my heart open. And like a child whose parents whisper loving words to it which it doesn't understand until it's a little older, I didn't really understand those words from the Gospel until later. I needed to hear the living Word. I needed the loving words of God the Father to help me feel even before I could understand and to realise that I was loved, that I had always been loved and that now it was my turn to love.

211

All the structures of liberty do not make a man free.

212

Jesus on the cross had none of the 'freedoms' for which men struggle. Yet he was truly free. True freedom is man's ability — which nothing and no one can take away from him — to accept or refuse the heaviest of burdens.

213

Only love can bring true freedom; in the struggle for freedom, only love can build a truly free man and world.

214

I've been to see X. I hadn't seen him for a while and we had a few things to talk about. He's always glad to see me, I give him an excuse to dine out. 'Let's go out to dinner, my treat,' he'll say. I accept, smiling to myself, as I see his barely concealed delight when he orders a good little wine and waves aside my protestations with a 'Let me — just this once.' And I'm happy because he's happy.

I should dine more often with my friends. It's just that I feel I'm wasting time, but is it wasted time? I'm sure Jesus had better things to do than to go and drink at a wedding in Cana, but he went all the same.

You're right, Lord. I will dine with those I love and with others when I get to know them better. But do have pity on my liver!

215

I've just returned from a two-day course of study. We were about thirty people and we talked a lot. Two days per person, multiplied by thirty people, that's sixty days of work right there, sacrificed for the sake of 'meditation', not counting the cost of the two days: two months' salary plus fees. Anyway, the exchanges were good. Towards the end, a bit tired after all that talking, I said: 'Now, in *practical* terms, what are we going to do?' Silent astonishment. One annoyed person said: 'Practical, practical, it's always got to be practical.' Well, it's just that I'm a practical person. Perhaps I should have kept quiet. But then, why should I? Too bad if it made me unpopular! What, after all, did I say that was so wrong? All I wanted was to see the thinking and meditating put into action. I threw a pebble into the still pool of our good conscience and caused a fierce little ripple in the general euphoric satisfaction by suggesting that now was the time to *act*.

216

While overseas (but it could have been right here at home), I was asked to sit in on a meeting. I did and mostly I listened. Then, the more I heard, the more my little interior demon (of course, it could also have been my guardian angel) got worked up. As usual, it pushed me to the point where I could hardly sit still. The work in hand concerned the composition of pastoral guidelines for an important region of the country, yet much time was being lost in futile, stubborn talk. They just weren't agreeing; some were completely opposed to one another, a few tried to smooth out the differences, but mostly they all stuck to their own opinions about the content and wording of the guidelines. Time was passing and already they were talking about the need for a second meeting, since they hadn't accomplished much at this one. Cigarette smoke filled the room — a sign of tension and intense activity. Things progressed at a snail's pace; now they were fighting over sentences and words. 'That's the wording I want and it's going to stay!' 'No it's not, you're all wrong.' And so on and on. Word after word was defended, disputed, torn to bits.

After dinner that evening we continued. That's when I was asked to intervene. I was distant enough to be objective and when I spoke, they all listened carefully (I was impressed!). I felt that I could perhaps have them begin at the beginning and on the right foot this time. On the other hand, I also felt that my suggestions might be as futile as the previous meeting. Still, I voiced the question that had been buzzing around in my head all day: 'What are you going to do with this text once it's written?'

'It's going to be copied and distributed to priests and laymen.'

'And then?'

'They'll discuss it among themselves.'

'And then?'

'Well, they'll give their opinions, make proposals for amendments if necessary, and so on.'

'And then?'

'We'll amend the text, taking into account all the suggestions we receive.'

'And then?'

'We'll have a final version of it. It'll then be printed and distributed.'

'And then . . .?'

The person I was talking with seemed suddenly disarmed. He didn't answer. 'Are you sure it's going to be read?' I insisted. 'How will you make sure it is? How is it going to be applied? Will it be applied correctly? By whom? How will you verify it? What will you do about any problems that might arise? How will you deal with delays, opposition, whatever?'

Silence. I felt as if I were speaking another language. When it comes to action, things break down. Honourable people stripped of their words are helpless. What a contrast between the profusion of ideas, the grim discussions, the self-confidence of the day and the embarrassed silence of this evening. Again I am aware of the enormous gap between concept and realisation.

After a few calm exchanges, the person in charge said humbly: 'Father Quoist is right, we must think about the problems that may arise, we must look beyond the writing of this text. I propose we organise a committee to *think* about it. . . .'

I left them arguing about who should be on the committee. Tempers were rising once again.

All that time and energy down the drain! Maybe I was harsh with them, but I knew exactly what would happen to that text. It would be painstakingly put together by sociologists, psychologists, an army of specialists; it would be read, reviewed, criticised, amended, re-written . . . and then shelved. In fact, three years later I asked to see this document that was going to revolutionise pastoral methods. 'Which one's that?' they asked. What! Had they forgotten it already? I asked the man in charge about it, describing it in detail. 'Oh that one!' he exclaimed. 'Why, it's been outdated for ages!'

217

Think hard about what you're doing. Think about what you could be doing. But don't waste time thinking about what you can't do, because you'll eventually end up believing that you can do what you can't and you'll build your life on a tragic illusion.

218

There's no shortage of teachers to instruct you on what should be done. But there are very few who can teach you *how* to do it. Most teachers wouldn't know — they've never done it.

219

The way things are going, who's going to want to be a religious or become a priest? Who's going to dedicate his life to God and mankind, in a positive state of celibacy? Who could be called on to go among the youth of today — 'modern' as they are, with their bodies and hearts 'liberated', who've understood that to love means loving with all one's being, that is, to *live* their love not only with their heart and soul but also with their body — and who realise sooner or later that this love is no less beautiful than spiritual love?

I ask myself this question when I notice that if one dug into certain past vocations, one would find much fear, taboos, value judgments and even contempt at the root of this famous celibacy. In short, a lot of hidden repression. Certainly young people, some of them handicapped, still come to the Church; but I do wish that the people in charge, in spite of being worried about the lack of applicants to the priesthood, would have the courage and lucidity to turn them down.

The youth of today more than ever have a good overall healthy idea of love; they have no illusions about the sacrifice they'll be making by dedicating their lives to God and others. They know they will be living this love, but expressing it in different ways. They need to be passionate about this love; not a love of God 'up there somewhere', but of God incarnate, made man in Jesus Christ and the Church, here on earth, existing here and now.

220

Severed ties always create anguish. Think how a spider panics when one of the strands of its cobweb is broken. In the same way people panic and suffer when their ties with nature, with other people, with God, are broken. They lose their sense of security. They're cut off from their lifeline. Hurt and frightened, they lose their self control. Like ship-wrecked people they frantically search for something to hold on to — but there's nothing strong enough to carry their weight, so they drown.

Man's ties must be remade.

221

If your roots are firmly planted, be sure you know what you're doing before pulling them up and moving on. A plant always suffers when transplanted; it needs time to grow more roots and time to develop before it can bear any fruit.

222

We waste so much time in remorse; we're slaves to guilt, disappointed in ourselves, humiliated. There's really only one thing worth doing and that is getting up and running to the Father, believing truly that he awaits us.

Let us offer him what he wants most — the return of his children. Let us prove to him that whatever our infidelities, we still believe in his love. Being a sinner isn't that serious.

What is serious is to continue in sin instead of running to the Father. Let us not delay it one more second!

223

This afternoon I met some admirably sincere Christians. Having told me how they constantly strive to 'deepen their faith and develop their union with the Lord', they went on to tell me that they could only give what they had and that they had to 'resource' themselves before 'going towards others'. While I admired their convictions, I was nevertheless divided and vaguely embarrassed. Despite their apparent humility, I gradually began to see them as rich and arrogant people. They were so sure that they had been chosen (and were able) to 'bring God to others'. I suddenly understood my unease. They were proving something I'd been saying for a long time — they really, sincerely, thought that you could 'possess God and pass him on to the Godless' and the more you had, the more you could give. It was horrible! There was the nub of that subtle arrogance which I had always suspected — the worst arrogance of all, that of believing we are rich with God while others aren't.

No one can 'possess' God. All we can do is to open ourselves to his love and let ourselves be loved. No one can give God to others. God gives himself to those he loves — that is, *everyone*. We don't have to 'go towards others', we're already with them. On the contrary, we have to assess our own worth in the eyes of others, through Christ's love and turn to God who awaits us in each of our brothers.

224

I prefer people who don't share my ideas but who are at least doing something, to those who share my ideas and do nothing at all.

225

Consider first what they're capable of, then suggest they do it. Don't just tell them what they should be doing — that'll only turn them off.

226

Thinkers sometimes look on doers with pity. Things are always easier and more attractive in the mind. . . .

227

She's just left my office. She's what they call an 'active' Christian. I asked her what she did at work and in her leisure time. She told me. Then I asked, 'What else do you do?' She replied, 'I'm very involved in a study group.' I asked what group she meant, who was in it, how often it met, what they had studied during the year. She said they'd studied the work of the Church.

'All year long?'

'Yes'.

'And then what?'

'Well . . . and then . . . why, we went on to something else!'

And there you have it — a whole year just to think about the Church's work. I don't know what they talked about, but I can imagine: lay people should have a larger role in the functions of the Church and they should be recognised for it; priests tend to have too much control; it's not right; and so on.

I'm sure both the group and the discussions were serious. I'm sure all aspects, such as history and theology, were covered. The woman I was talking to is a demanding person and she proved it. She was quite harsh on the subject of people who 'don't think ahead or far enough'. I let her speak — in fact, I couldn't stop her. She *knew* what had to be done, she had *thought* about it. And she continues to think . . . with her friends.

Oh yes, a very 'active' Christian indeed!

228

What undermines the authority of officials is the gap between the importance of their plans and the modesty of their realisation, if indeed there is any.

It's no good having ideas if you can't follow them through. If you want to be taken seriously your plans must be realistic enough to be put into practice. Do you have the manpower, the means, the time? Evaluate all obstacles and opposition. Then, while you may end up doing things piecemeal, you'll at least be carrying out, rather than admiring, your idea on paper.

Don't leave yourself hanging in mid-air.

229

I just heard about a man who tinkered away at a motorcycle and put together such an overblown, formidable engine that when he finally went to try it out, it wouldn't budge.

We're all becoming do-it-yourselfers, tinkering, rebuilding and perfecting our cars — which we keep locked up in our garages. We thrill to the sound of purring engines or sudden acceleration. Our silence is filled with noises that flatter us, and others admire us for being able to create them. But none of this puts us in the right gear. Our car just sits in the garage, we lock the doors . . . until the next noise session.

The same thing happens to the mind if it's not in the 'right gear', if it's not focused on reality. That's one of the problems with society today — the gap between man's great ideas and possibilities and the limits of their realisation.

230

We need scholars, real ones. But genuine intellectual work requires asceticism and effort, both of which are rare. In fact many people just skim through different fields of knowledge, call themselves 'specialists' and propagate a pseudo-science — a badly digested mish-mash — to fit in with preconceived ideas. Partial knowledge engenders illusion and stupidity; it can also discourage real study.

231

We live in a talkative world. These are times of tired words and hackneyed phrases which sap the energies of those who speak them and leave them too anaemic to act. There is a compulsion to hold meetings, seminars, week-end sessions; there is all manner of intellectual self-indulgence as one sits and thinks about problems. This sort of thing betrays a serious inability to act and this is modern man's scourge. So he compensates by resorting to pseudo-intellectualism. You could call it a collective schizophrenia. The Church in France hasn't escaped it either. It thinks and thinks and thinks.

232

I don't have the time! We don't have the time!

It's not true. We don't *take* the time. We let life gnaw away at our time, stealing it from us bit by bit. We're slaves, not masters.

We must be masters of our time.

I must control my life — and the obligations it imposes on me — not the other way around.

233

The only 'road to heaven' is the earth itself. Every step I take on earth leads me to heaven: the steps I take today, on this earth where I live, surrounded by people, in my own community and my environment.

No road exists in my imagination or good ideas. My road is the earth and only my feet can take me anywhere.

234

Tomorrow morning I'm due to give a talk in Tokyo. I'm already in the city so I can take it easy — I won't have far to go.

Well, that's what I thought. It turns out that I have to set off at 7.30 a.m. (I'm due to speak at 10). I'd forgotten that Tokyo is about 80 to 90 kilometres long. I'm going to have to travel by underground, train, a second train and finally a taxi.

The city of Tokyo, like all of Japan, is at once beautiful and monstrous. What they've accomplished here is admirable and worrying. The city is growing upwards — a network of highways is suspended overhead. It's also growing downwards — below ground level. Several levels of shopping malls offer everything people could ever want and need for life in the year 2000 — restaurants, bars, boutiques, banks, bookstores. The whole country is a reflection of its capital city.

I rode in what was at the time the fastest train in the world, 200 km an hour. Nothing, not mountains or valleys or the sea prevents its advance — man has truly conquered nature. Soon, I'm told, there will be an underwater tunnel beside which the one proposed below the English Channel will pale, while in other areas the sea is being pushed back to make way for man-made islands.

Here is a whole nation at work. One has to be impressed at the genius of the Japanese. Nothing daunts them. But from the moment I stepped into their country, I was haunted by the image of a tower of Babel (they wanted to build a tower that would reach the sky!).

I admire the Japanese, but they frighten me. I was brave enough to tell them how I felt. Did I stress it enough?

235

For the fifth or sixth time, someone's brought up something I said on a previous trip to Japan.

Standing rather than sitting in the beautiful armchair which was reserved for me, I had said to my Japanese audience: 'You spend so much time making beautiful armchairs such as this one that you don't have the time to sit in them!' They had laughed, in that charming way they have when they're relaxed and at ease. And they didn't forget my remark — it seems they often refer to 'Father Quoist's armchair'. Long after they've forgotten my talk at the conference held at Sophia University in Tokyo, I think they'll still remember the imagery and idea of the armchair!!

I mustn't give in to the temptations of comic(?) opera when I should be concentrating on the aria.

236

I'm impressed by the number of people who come to my lectures (in Japan). I speak of Jesus Christ and they're not even Christians. But they listen; they ask questions. I'm told they find the idea of Jesus Christ attractive. Some have said to me: 'If I had to choose a religion, I would choose Christianity.

It's the most appealing!' That's precisely the problem: for them, Christianity is just a 'religion' among others. When will we be able to live, talk about and reveal Jesus Christ without bringing in 'religion'? Lord, I don't want to be a company agent, not even a religious company agent. I want to speak of your presence in our lives. But my name isn't Paul (it is no longer I who live but Christ who lives in me!). My name is Michel and despite the posters announcing me in bold characters, I often have an intense desire to write my name with a lower-case 'm'.

237

Japan definitely fascinates me. I'm fascinated because it is a place that reveals itself only very gradually. Who can truly understand this great people, so stifled on their little islands that they have to go out and conquer the world. But the world isn't large enough for them to find what they want. What are the Japanese looking for? They don't know. Why all this work, this gigantic effort to dominate the material? What is the *meaning* of their lives, the world, mankind? In their tiny world, everything is too large for them.

238

A Japanese seminarian told me, 'The Japanese are an anguished people, but they don't know why.' That's precisely what I'd thought myself.

MY JAPANESE FRIEND

I came to see you, Japanese friend
And loved you

I saw your face behind the door
Which you slowly opened, offering me your wonderful
smile
But what is behind that wonderful smile?
A Japanese garden
Magnificent, but closed
Closed for you, for others
Even more so for me, too long a stranger.

Who are you, Japanese friend?
You no longer have the time to look at yourself
You no longer have the time to commune with yourself.
When you return home late at night
Your door is shut
And you stay behind it.

What are you doing, Japanese friend?
With your steel, and the steel of your machines
Machines to conquer the world with!
But on your soil, Japanese friend
There is no space left for the cherry tree to blossom.

They tell me you're alone, Japanese friend.
Your garden is beautiful but few enter it.
You run so fast to buy the world, that you lose the key to
your garden.

Who are you, Japanese friend?
Why are you so alone, and without a key to your garden?

You're searching — for what?
You're waiting — for what?
You don't know, as you stand there, anguished
Under your artificial cherry tree*
While children are dying at your garden gate†

Listen to me, Japanese friend.
I know what you're waiting for
And I know who you're waiting for.
The one you're waiting for holds the key to your garden.

239

Man has only just been born. I'm sure of that. He's a baby; he's
still babbling. In him a tiny speck of awareness has surfaced,
hiding a more or less infinite sea of subconsciousness which
he still has to penetrate. When he does, he will have grown up.
It's quite a wonderful adventure when you think of it.

In their search for God, mystics (Oriental and Western) have
glimpsed something of the paths in a prodigious hinterland.

*There are very few real cherry trees in Japan today. Whole streets are lined
with paper ones.
†Refers to child suicide — not uncommon in Japan.

And by walking down these paths with vision, they have become better men by becoming more god-like.

These days, many of our contemporaries have discovered their 'interior paths'. But their pride gets in the way and they lose their bearings. They want to become 'new men', 'supermen' and they want to do it alone: 'You will be like Gods!'

Psychoanalysts, in a general fashion, undertake this exploration of the subconscious with great enthusiasm. They perceive a mysterious world wherein lies a fabulous energy, which they awaken but can't always control. They play at being sorcerers' apprentices.

The meditators (transcendental, zen, etc.), who are growing in numbers, are also foraying into the subconscious, in a dimension that can neither be denied nor forgotten. Still, the fact remains that they are proceeding *outside of all religion.*

Man is great, greater than he thinks, but he cannot grow alone. These days there is a cruel shortage of *Christian* mystics.

240

Decidedly my Japanese friends are of an extraordinary sensitivity. I had wanted to visit a Zen monastery, so they took me into the mountains to visit Father Lasalle (a German Jesuit who has lived most of his life in Japan studying Zen Buddhism, the subject of several of his books). I spent a day talking with him and the 'retreatees'.

At first glance, the place was no different from any Christian monastery, except for the meditation room, with a rock in the middle and a dais along the walls. There, people in retreat meditate facing the wall, seated in the lotus position (the only one in Zen). The monastery itself is starkly simple, but in a magnificent setting.

I think Father Lasalle said that the people in retreat met nine times a day to meditate for forty minutes, more or less. Meditation isn't something you can measure exactly. The Zen continues through mealtimes, walks, sleep. . . . All life is Zen.

The goal of this interior voyage is to attain and live on a level of intuitive awareness — deeper, more peaceful and infinitely more vast and powerful than conceptual awareness.

To transcend the thoughts and images which block the

way, the meditator uses a 'mantra' (a sacred word which often has no meaning, given him by his master, which he repeats to the rhythm of his breaking) and a 'mandela' (visual image) of, for example, a sound.

The voyage has no bounds, just stages. Some reach a stage where they are united to all their brothers and the whole universe by mysterious bonds. This is the true dimension of total manhood for them. One day they will also perhaps attain an indescribable 'illumination' that, it seems, only those who have experienced it can comprehend.

You have to be impressed. I was. But I still had a few questions; two in particular.

First: practised in this way, isn't Zen really just a luxury available to a handful of people? Father Lasalle set me straight. Many Japanese, including young people, dedicate a certain period of time to retreats in places like Buddhist temples, as a matter of course. In fact, a great number of people practise Zen in varying degrees.

Second, isn't this just an escape from reality, a sort of refuge? On the contrary, affirmed Father Lasalle, they return to their normal lives more aware and mentally more alert than before.

I observed Father Lasalle. He is the living answer to my questions. The great Zen master radiates peace, gentleness and goodness. The quality and sensitivity of his attention reveal a total presence. He's not disembodied, he's reincarnated.

I left more than ever convinced that most of us live below the surface of our lives. We are under-developed.

241

A beaming child gave me a smooth pebble that he'd picked specially for me. I thanked him warmly.

Eight days later, the child asked: 'What have you done with my pebble?'

I just couldn't tell him I'd thrown it away. So I lied.

242

I'm happy to see flowers on my desk. But I'd rather have only a few, perhaps just one. I don't have the time to love them all.

243

Did you say you didn't know how to pray? Don't worry. The apostles who travelled with Jesus didn't know how to pray either. They asked him to teach them how.

You say it's difficult to pray and often you're bored with it? Don't worry. When the Lord in his anguish waited for the comfort of their prayers, the apostles were . . . sleeping.

244

I like this definition of prayer by C. de Hueck Doherty: 'a contract of love between God and man.' Prayer involves a meeting of people in the spirit of love. And there are as many ways of loving and expressing one's love as there are prayers.

DO YOU WANT TO KNOW WHAT PRAYER IS ALL ABOUT, LITTLE ONE? LISTEN.
'If anyone loves me he will keep my word, and my Father will love him, and we shall come to him and *make our home with him*' (John 14:23).
'But when you pray, go to your private room and, when you have shut the door, pray to your Father who is in that secret place . . .' (Matthew 6:6).
Do you want to know what prayer is all about, little one? Listen.

When you pray, you go to meet the King. The King, of course, lives in a castle. But this King owns many castles. His castles aren't in the clouds, the way they are in fairytales; they're built right here on earth. I'm going to tell you a secret. It's not really a secret because it's written in the Book, but people today no longer read the Book. The King loves everyone and he loves them so much that just to be near them, he built a castle in each person's heart. What's even better is that he can live in all his castles all at once. That way he makes sure you won't miss him.

To enter the castle you must go through the door. Some go in through the windows (well, they're just bad mannered) but the King is so good that he receives them anyway. In fact, they say that he gets even more enjoyment out of this lot! He laughs and says to them: 'What funny little acrobats you are!' And he embraces them more warmly than the others. But you, you're well behaved so you'll enter through the door — well, one of the doors anyway, because there are several.

To reach the castle at the centre of your heart, you can enter through *the door of your body*. There are many people who just borrow it; they put their body on its knees (but this is outmoded); they lie flat on their faces; they lie on their backs, with a rug underneath them — it's more comfortable. They sit silent and motionless in some rather strange positions. After some time they declare that they've met the King. You can tell them that they're wrong, because they haven't moved from the entrance to their bodies. The King is very touched by their efforts but he's waiting deep inside the castle, far beyond the entrance.

To reach the castle at the centre of your heart, you can also take *the door of your emotions*. You know, 'emotion' means when you're happy all over, inside, because you're looking at something beautiful, because someone's nice to you, because you love somebody. . . . Many people like this door. To be really happy inside, these people often assemble in a lovely room and light candles. If the candles are coloured ones, they're even happier. They gaze at a painting. It's got a funny name — icon — and it often comes from Russia (but don't worry, it's not Communist!). They hold one another's hands or they embrace; they're happier when they embrace. Some sing, others talk. They talk so much that they can't stop. They speak beautiful words and sometimes, words we can't understand. So those who do understand explain the words to the rest of us. In short, they're very very nice, very very happy people. They smile a lot and say, 'We have met the King.' You can tell them they're wrong because they haven't moved from the entrance to their emotions. The King is very touched by their efforts but he's waiting deep inside the castle, far beyond the entrance.

To reach the castle at the centre of your heart, you can also go through *the door of your mind*. A lot of people enter this way. They read books; they come upon ideas in them, then they close their eyes and try to imagine these ideas, because you don't see ideas with the eyes of the body, you see them with the eyes of the mind. Special eyes to see ideas with. When these ideas are used up, they go back to the books for more. The most intelligent find ideas on their own, beautiful ideas, ideas on the King. Others chase ideas, turning them over and over in their minds. Some ideas are so beautiful that they sit and look at them for the longest time. Then they open their eyes and say, 'We have seen the King!' You can tell them they're wrong, because they haven't moved from the entrance to their minds. The King is very touched by their efforts but he's waiting deep inside the castle, far beyond the entrance.

Do you understand, little one, a door is made to be entered. If you just stand there in front of it, you'll never see the inside of the castle and you'll never meet the King, because the King lives deep within it.

If you decide to go in, 'shut the door', as the Book says. Because a door is made to be shut behind you.

Listen, little one, do you really want to continue on this path? Do you really want to walk towards the King? It's difficult, you know, because once you've shut the door, you'll be in darkness and silence. A lot of people can't bear it. They say to themselves, 'I made a mistake, I'm wasting my time here — *there's no one here*' and they retreat hastily to look for another entrance. Tell them they're wrong — there's darkness and silence behind *every* door. And so, many people just stand there, outside the doors of the castle. . . .

You, little one, are brave, you *believe*. You believe that the King is in the castle. You believe that he's waiting for you. You believe that he loves you, because he said so. Continue walking and don't be afraid of anything. If you *believe*, the Spirit of the King will come to you. He'll take you by the hand and guide you and one day he'll say to you: 'That's where it is.' You won't see or hear anything, you won't even feel anything, but the voice of your heart will say, 'I believe, I believe, I believe, in the darkness and the silence.'

Then you'll know that the King is there. He will kiss you and that kiss, my child, is not something I can explain to you. All I can say is that you'll never ever forget it.

245

Words, gestures, feelings and thoughts of love are not love itself, merely conveyors of a mystery beyond comprehension. In the same way, thoughts, emotions and gestures are only paths through which we can attain Him who is the infinite present — and present beyond the subconscious beyond.

246

I used to dislike the term 'to recollect' as in 'to recollect oneself'. I thought it tired and deformed; it reminded me of angular, grey faces perched above scrawny necks more precarious than the tower of Pisa. But I rediscovered the term and find it quite marvellous now.

To recollect yourself is to recover all your scattered energies — those of the mind, the heart and body. It is to reassemble all the pieces of yourself flung in the four corners of your past or the mists of your future, pieces clinging to the fringes of your desires. It is to put all yourself in your words, gestures, smiles, kisses and embraces and to go, thus enriched *of yourself*, to others and to God.

247

Yet another young person telling me he didn't choose to be born! Well, he's right — we don't choose to be born. However, a person can't build a healthy self if he doesn't accept, deep down, the life that's been 'imposed' on him. It's easier if it was given through love, but harder if the child was carried for nine months in a body that gave it physical nourishment but emotional rejection — 'If only it would die and free us!'

I know that many use the argument, 'Only wanted babies should be brought into this world,' to justify abortion, but it's hardly as simple as that. A baby could be wanted as a toy, or something that might save a floundering marriage, or to assure happiness in old age! It's not easy to *give* life freely to children without wanting to take it back in one way or another.

248

We've entered the era not only of individual suicide (it is increasing) but of the suicide of the species. In certain countries where the population is declining you may soon have to pay people to have children and if the fee is high enough they might just produce one. The psychoanalysts will do well out of it, to be sure! Their patients used to be people who were scarred because they were unwanted, considered 'accidents' by their parents. In future years some may suffer the same traumatic scars but for different reasons — they were born for a fee, a price. When they've reached their teens, what with devaluation, they'll discover how cheaply they were 'bought'.

249

God incarnated himself in Jesus Christ. Many people spend their time denying his incarnation. They search in the sky and miss him right here on earth, where he is to be found in their daily lives.

250

Many right-thinking people haven't accepted the incarnation. They can't admit that God didn't 'keep his place'. And when they do, they want you to think that it's just a passing whim, that they'll get over it. . . . Christ came to earth on a mission, accomplished it quickly and perfectly and rejoined his Father — up there.

There's no shortage of Christians to guide Christ to the elevator, shut the door and press the button. There! Off he goes, back to heaven, where he belongs. It's much more convenient this way, definitely more practical. He'll be off our streets now.

251

X. says he believes in Jesus Christ. But he considers Christ a prophet, the greatest of them all; a wise man who should be heeded, a model who should be imitated.

I congratulate him. Fine, continue, follow Jesus Christ. He can't believe his ears.

'But . . . you don't. . . .'

'We're not talking about me. You've met him, you believe he's a good 'shepherd'. Walk with him. I'll tell you this much — it's not going to be easy.'

X. is generous and faithful. He tries to live the Gospel. I know that some day, sooner or later, Christ will show him his identity card.

I meet many young people like X. I love and admire them. Sometimes I find them more generous than myself. But am I close enough to them to reveal, when the moment comes, the real name of the man they're following?

252

Over dinner with some friends we got into a discussion that began turning into an argument. They all professed to be Christians, but in fact their understanding of Christianity and their way of life diverged completely. I was obliged to play Solomon, a role I dislike. I'm sure that some of them felt misunderstood, but they stuck to their opinions.

These people, in fact, fall into two groups — I may be simplifying here, but I think the distinction is clear. The first group believes Jesus Christ died and was resurrected, but to 'heaven', into the clouds, who knows where! In any case, very far from earth. Theirs is a 'remembrance religion' — Christ came here 2,000 years ago, then died; past history. Later, we'll be reunited with him when he 'calls us home'.

The second group believes in the resurrected Christ, but believes he is living among us today. He continues to be born, live, suffer and die in his followers. He is part of everyone; the mystery of his love continues timelessly. His disciples rejoin him in life to continue and complete his mission of the liberation of mankind and the universe. Faith then becomes a lifelong commitment.

Jesus continues to ask you and me: Who am I for you?

253

Every act of true love (*act*, not sentiment) by man, Christian or not, enables the love of God to reach the heart of the world and slowly fill it. God is present in all acts of love; this is how Christ is born — gradually, growing to his 'full adult height'.

I still recall my enthusiasm when, having met Jesus Christ (I was still working in an office in those days), I read in the first letter of St John that all love comes from God! I used to think about that at work, trying hard to love, telling myself: God is present in every gesture of love, just as the sun is present in every ray that shines out of it. I must let the sun shine!

254

The omnipotence of God expresses itself solely in the weakness of love. On the cross no 'human strength' remains except love. This radical weakness is necessary to give man total freedom.

255

In ancient times people invoked fire from the heavens to consummate their sacrifices. I invoke the fire of love to burn in every moment of my life. But I'm not an ancient sacrifice, an animal, a victim to be offered up. I am — no, I would *like to be* — a lover who gives himself.

256

Meeting Christ — putting yourself completely in his hands — doesn't involve depersonalisation but, on the contrary, 'super-personalisation'.

257

I wanted to see one of these youth communities which are flourishing all over the United States and Canada (and now, in France). While on a visit to Canada, I was lucky enough to have the time, for a change, to go and visit one.

I spent a day at a place called the Community of Saint Francis, where about fifty young men and women in their mid-twenties live in two wooden cabins in the forest — one for the men, the other for the women. During the day they eat, work, pray and meditate together.

All of them have travelled practically all over the world (including the obligatory trip to India!) and experienced all manner of drugs and sex. They've done it all. And some of them had become veritable wrecks.

Now they say they've met Jesus Christ, that they've been converted and have decided to dedicate their lives to the Lord. They're even considering taking vows to that effect.

They lead a life of concentrated prayer. Every morning, whatever the weather, they walk to the church in a nearby village for mass. The parishioners have got accustomed to seeing these strange-looking creatures — girls in long dresses, boys with long flowing hair — wearing large wooden crosses around their necks, who sit on the ground for hours praying silently after mass. They're likeable enough, they're discreet. 'We've nothing against them,' say the parishioners.

Then, in turn, without a penny in their pockets, they take to the road in twos to 'evangelise'. Sometimes they sing, accompanied by a guitar. They talk to passers-by on the streets, in supermarkets and they go to various schools and colleges where students come to listen to them. They announce Jesus Christ, they 'give witness'.

Peter arrives. He's their 'shepherd', the one who can best speak about the Bible and who guides them all. He's just returned from an evangelising session accompanied by a 'sister'. They're happy. They talk about it. Everyone bursts with joy and gives praise to the Lord.

I begin putting some questions to Peter in a straightforward fashion. I feel a bit ashamed, I feel like an investigating officer of the law, or an inquisitor looking for something he can condemn. In fact, these youngsters make me uneasy. They make me question myself and defend myself by being aggressive. Peter answers my questions quietly, in a gentle tone that contrasts with his tough woodsman's clothes. His patience is exemplary, his smile strong. His answers are simple and ring true. He's young — 27, perhaps 28 years old; he's travelled all over without knowing what he was looking for. Then one day he found the buried treasure, abandoned everything and went to live alone in a forest for a year, with the Word of God as his only companion.

I ask a few questions, the ones I feel are the most important. His answers speak for themselves.

'Peter, you say you're guided by a priest, that you trust him, that for you he's your bishop's spokesman. If he said to you tomorrow: "I've thought hard about what you're doing, I've prayed; I'm now quite sure that living this way is a mistake; you must stop", what would you do?'

'I would stop, I'd tell the brothers to stop and I would go off alone again, to pray, to ask the Holy Spirit to enlighten me.'

'Before you returned, your friends told me that you'd gone very far in your experiences with meditation. At the moment you pray two hours a day. What's the difference?'

'Yes I did go very far in meditation and concentration. I studied transcendental meditation with specialists. I think I've attained levels of the subconscious that not many have experienced. It's true that what I'm doing now may seem exactly the same, but my goal is different. Before, I searched and searched but I only kept bumping into myself. Now I'm going towards Someone.'

Peter passed the test. He told me what I wanted to know. We spoke a little longer and I left. The brothers and sisters praised the Lord for Michel this and Michel that. I was a bit embarrassed. I began to wonder if I wasn't the one who should be doing all the thanking!

When I returned home, I discussed it with my colleagues. Most of them didn't know quite what to make of it. They didn't want to 'judge'. One priest didn't hesitate though: 'They've replaced one drug with another,' he shrugged. Perhaps, but this drug has done wonders for them and they don't need doctors and psychiatrists, or other admirable people who by their own admission can't always help. I can make comparisons: in New York I saw a drug addict going through withdrawal pains rolling around in agony on the sidewalk. It was horrible! In Paris and London, I saw young addicts lining up outside pharmacies for their dose of methodone, the drug that would give them relief from their withdrawal pains. They fought savagely for first place in line. To be sure, the brothers and sisters of the Community are something else altogether. I think they really have met Someone.

They were transformed and full of joy. They want to shout their good news to the world and tell everyone of the One who saved them, so that their brothers will also welcome him. Can you blame them? I remember the priests in the early days of the Paris missions, the ones who were to become the first worker priests. The 'faithful' don't need to be told of Jesus Christ; it's the ones on the outside who need to be told. So they preached in the streets. I remember in particular certain stations of the cross I used to participate in — they took place in the *métro* (underground)! Worker priests have come a long way, so much that we forget how and where they started. Why be surprised? Do flowers and fruit resemble their roots? Roots, however, must be nurtured periodically. This afternoon I couldn't help thinking of the poor man of Assisi (since we're talking about the Community of St Francis), this hippie of the twelfth century taking to the roads, begging, announcing the Gospel. 'Right-thinking' and wise men called him mad and threw stones at him. Perhaps even I would have been more comfortable this afternoon had I been able to conclude that these young people were mad. Instead of stones, I'd have thrown some words of wisdom at them. I confess I was unable to. I was too impressed. They're not mad and if they are, *am I then mad enough?*

258

I was skimming through the newspaper when an item on an accident caught my eye. How sad, I thought and was about to turn the page when I saw the name of the victim. I was stunned — it was someone I knew. I telephoned mutual friends who confirmed that it was indeed him and that he was fatally injured. I didn't know what to say. This sort of thing usually happens to others; this time it had hit very close to home. But X. survived. He's going to be all right.

I thought about him for a long time. A tragic accident can be merely sad or tragic depending whether you know the victim or not. Sad if it's just a name in the paper; tragic if it's someone you know. That's how it is. We can't take on all the world's suffering. But is my heart large enough, or am I too far removed from my brothers?

Lord, who is my neighbour?

259

They said: 'We believe that Christ is alive and present among us but where can we be certain to find him?'

I replied: 'First, where he said he would be. It's easy, he left many addresses in the Gospel. Second, where life nurtures the Gospel.' I used the imagery I had discovered in Canada (No. 260 below). We looked for the addresses together and we found:

1. The community. From the two or three gathered together in the name of Jesus to the large community of the Church (given this condition, Jesus said he would be among us).

2. The heart of a man who loves his brothers. St John reminds us of the commandment on brotherly love and later quotes Jesus: 'If anyone loves me he will keep my word, and my Father will love him, and we shall come to him, and make our home with him' (John 14:23).

3. The signs Jesus left behind, especially the sharing of bread and wine. 'For I was hungry and you gave me food, I was thirsty and you gave me drink . . .' (Matthew 25:35–46).

Then, together, we searched for Jesus Christ in their *lives*. I noticed, as many times before, that some could truly 'see'. Too often I 'know', but to them Christ is revealing himself — they meet him before 'knowing'.

260

I had been told that to get to the city I would have to drive through a large forest (this was in Canada). I was looking forward to it, but when I got there I was really disappointed. I had expected tall, majestic trees and all I saw were puny little things that looked more like bushes. Nothing but bushes. It was quite dark and I kept thinking: 'There aren't any flowers!'

That evening, in the city, I said to my audience: 'Imagine you were walking through one of your large forests and among all those trees, you saw one perfect rose. You'd assume there was a rose bush there, so you'd stop and look for it and you'd find it. Do the same in life. Walk on but at the same time, look around you. Whenever you see the Gospel blooming, tell yourselves that Christ is there, present in his mysterious way, working with his Spirit to build a new man and a new world.'

Thus a Christian is not one who 'gives God to the world'; he is a believer of the Word (I will be among you to the end of time) who lives his life in the footsteps of Christ, recognises him and joins him in his work.

Faith is a commitment.

261

We must welcome the night. It's the only time that the stars shine.

262

I've always dreamed of solitude, the hermit's life, a cabin in the woods or a tiny chalet on the edge of a mountain. I've always dreamed of deserts and silence. But I've resisted the dream, with the exception of one time when I offered myself the luxury of a retreat with a hermit: four hours by foot, far from any living creature and a hermit happy to see me. We talked a lot.

I understood then that I carry my hermitage around with me and that I don't need to go too far to meet my Lord. I often need to withdraw into my retreat, if only for a few minutes. Christ waits for me there.

263

A parable for me and many others: a man had two friends, a man and a woman (who didn't know each other). He loved both his friends; they were very likeable people, but neither was married and both suffered terribly from loneliness. And both were wasting away.

The man thought: 'What if I introduce them to each other? Perhaps they'd like each other.' He wouldn't admit it, but he was quite sure they'd like each other. However, in the name of discretion, respect, not wanting to 'interfere' and so on, he let it slide and the two never met, never even knew the other existed. And the man still said nothing.

The two lonely people grew old, bitter and died in their solitude.

Christians are often like this man. We know Jesus Christ, we know that his love can illuminate lives and make them fruitful. But we don't divulge his name to those who search and struggle alone. We use 'discretion' as an excuse: 'When the Lord wills' and 'We must let things happen naturally,' and even 'They're not ready for it yet.'

Let's be honest. Isn't it because we're timid, rather than discreet? This is worse, because that means Jesus Christ is not one hundred per cent part of our lives and struggles. If we'd really met him, we couldn't possibly keep quiet about it!

264

Being virtuous doesn't preclude slipping up and falling, once in a while. Being virtuous means getting up and trying again.

265

'Love your neighbour as yourself.' What does it mean if not putting him first, if he is less fortunate than yourself, as Abbé Pierre puts it.

It's at once simple and frightening.

Given this definition, who can confidently say that he truly loves his brothers, the way Christ intended? So many lives are built on illusion! A few kind gestures, a commitment or two, and you have a good conscience. We give a little of our lives and we're so proud of ourselves. We place ourselves in the ranks of 'authentic Christians', but all we've given is a crumb or two.

As for me, what can I say for myself, I who have made a career of total giving?

266

I've been talking to some Trappist monks. I was in a humorous mood, wanting to laugh and make them laugh.

And so they did. I think you can measure the health, equilibrium and value of a community by its capacity for laughter.

I must admit I've rarely been disappointed. I've met many communities of nuns, for example, who literally went off into peals of laughter. Only once did the sisters hesitate, betraying only pale smiles despite what I was saying. Did they have the right to laugh, or not? They glanced furtively at their abbess. She just stood there, as rigid as Justice. Her closed face egged me on. I wanted to see her smile. She finally did, but with such reticence that she seemed to be offering us the fruits of defeat. But defeat or not, the sisters didn't get much out of it. Not as much as I would have liked them to anyway. I decided to denounce the community at the next conference of religious congregations in Rome! I never did, though — I was afraid the presiding cardinal might not laugh!

267

There is noise in silence. I already knew that, but I experienced it almost physically last night. It was overwhelming.

I went to bed very late. The whole house was asleep; so were the streets and the city. Not a sound. And yet words and ideas went round and round in my head and my heart like the traffic in rush hour: traffic jams, honking, shouts, exasperation. I decided to stop this racket. Eyes shut, I concentrated on my breathing. I breathed deeply, slowly. I felt life penetrating me: communion with nature, the vital link with the universe. And one by one the noises disappeared, the silence was silent once again and I felt God move faintly. He was there. I said good morning and good night to him and went to sleep.

There is definitely noise in silence.

268

Allow others their differences — indeed, help them. An easy thing to say but, in fact, we are loath to let others be themselves; we want them to be like us. It's a sort of deviation, even perversion, of the human being. And it's the most serious of deviations.

269

My freedom allows me to recollect myself completely so that I can be waiting for LOVE uncreated, be penetrated by that LOVE, transformed by it. I become a place where LOVE eternal is concentrated. A place of incarnation.

270

I missed the flight. Now I have to wait for the next one. I don't mind. I can sit here and watch people; I can write.

I always feel quite alone in international airports, these modern Babylons where people of all nations pass each other but never meet. Except, of course, if they're lovers.

I look at lovers, I like watching them. They're always in airports, on railway platforms, at bus stations. They look at the time anxiously, they grow silent; it's nearly time to part and they can't find the words to express their feelings. Their gestures are tender, sometimes embarrassed under the harsh lights with all those eyes around them. They wait for the final announcement which they at once dread and welcome. And it comes, indifferent, soul-less, to wrench the lovers apart. But they fight it; they cling to each other, they kiss — a loving kiss so beautiful, so rich when it is really meant. It says more than any words can say: 'I don't want to leave you, I want you to come with me, I can't bear to be without you.' And then the giving of the self, in communion, one to the other: 'Go my darling, go. I'll always be with you. We'll always be together.'

We humans have invented gestures rich with meaning; sacraments of daily life for our hungering brothers. We have invented the handshake to transmit friendship, and the kiss to give our love with. But, imperfect and scattered as we are, our hearts are not completely in these gestures. Who can say that he makes them wholeheartedly? The sign is no longer always meaningful; and diverted, it can even become a counter-sign.

I think of you, Jesus, who couldn't bear the idea of leaving us. You, in total solidarity with man, the perfect lover, at the end of the terrestrial platform. You made a gesture — the sharing of bread and wine — and through it you said: 'I renew my alliance. I give myself to the Father and I give myself to you.' You, Jesus, put your entire being into that gesture and you made us a promise — that every time we re-enact it, you will be among us in a real, total way. And we will enter into communion with one another and become, together, the Body which must continue to grow to the end of time.

I look at the lovers around me, not in envy (though it does happen) but in gratitude. I thank you for your long kiss of love, Lord, which you perpetually offer all humanity . . . to the end of time.

The ones here have noticed me looking at them. I smile. They smile back.

Lord, thank them for me and let my smile be for them a 'sacrament'.

271

He wants me to find him some premises — 'I can't do a thing for these youngsters without a place to do it in,' he said.

You have to wonder about people who can't do a thing for the community unless they have 'premises' to do it in. Let's erect a building first, then we'll decide how to use it. I don't follow this logic.

People like these remind me of a man deploying tremendous efforts to construct, say, a magnificent canal system, then sitting back and waiting for the water to come along and fill it up. He's liable to be kept waiting an awfully long time!

Begin with the source; dig and find it. Then perhaps you can build your canals. And if the source is abundant, all the better. But be careful — as soon as the source is found, many water diviners leap in and start building on the assumption that there's plenty of water there. They end up abandoning the source, which in turn dries up when they're not looking!

272

There are plenty of canal builders around, but few source finders. It's not enough to have a divining rod to discover a source; you need to be gifted as well (by the Holy Spirit!).

You have a right to ask for this gift. A gift is always free. You must ask for it — have you asked often enough? Are you looking in the right places? The most magnificent projects, the most beautiful structures can never get water to spring forth.

Dig your daily earth. Dig where you step. Keep on digging, and have faith.

273

If he didn't tell you what was on his mind it was because he didn't feel he could.

You think he was afraid. In a way that's true, but if he was afraid, it was because you weren't really inviting, you weren't 'empty' enough, loving enough, to receive him.

Listening isn't easy! And yet, I'm fairly sure that people are overflowing with words, and in allowing them to express themselves, we allow them a measure of release, and a chance to become themselves again.

274

They are 'building' for their children. But are they really? In fact, what they want are children made of stone — once built, they're solid, they don't move.

We priests 'build' for God. But do we really? In fact, we too want children of stone, especially as we cannot have real flesh and blood ones.

(*Building* can also mean *doing*.)

275

They came to discuss their forthcoming wedding. After a long talk, I asked: 'Do you want to have children?' The answer was: 'Yes, one, but not right away. We need a new car first,' (this is a direct quotation!).

I was tempted to be very harsh, but I controlled myself. I must see this young couple again and find out what they really meant. But I immediately wrote down their answer to my question. It's too common unfortunately — a child today is more or less considered an *object*.

A baby is a sweet little thing. Every home should have one. It's good for both the husband and the wife. It assures their future. So let's make a list of indispensable things; mind you, a dog would be cheaper and easier to take care of. And so affectionate towards his mama and dada!

A world in which a child becomes an object is a world in danger.

276

In a homily delivered on television, I said: 'Parents, you claim you've given life to your children. Are you sure? If you've really "given" it, then don't try to take it back, to pluck it back by the heart.'

The response (a positive one) was overwhelming. Parents said: 'You're so right, and it's so difficult.'

I agree. In fact, I think it's harder to *really* love your children than your spouse.

In a marriage, a husband tries to give everything to his wife, but he also receives everything she tries to give him, and vice versa. Parents, together, must gradually offer their children the life they themselves received. And their children will give them nothing in return, not directly, because they in turn will give their life to someone else: a stranger.

277

Children should thank their parents for the life they've been given (they could have chosen not to give them life at all!), but they must take charge of this life and lead it. In turn they must hand their life to their children, who will pass it on to theirs, and so on.

Those who cling to their life, or try to take back any they've given, cause it to die.

Children shouldn't rush to give a few strands of their life to their parents. Instead, they should tell them, and show them, what they've done with this gift: 'Look what we've done with your gift of love; look at our marriage, our children, our commitments, our lives. What you have *given* us has borne fruit. Be happy and proud!'

But be careful that parents don't pick this fruit — *it is not theirs to take!*

278

I've been travelling again, this time for myself. It's probably the only time I've solicited an invitation myself. It wasn't a success. It wasn't too bad, but there's a bad taste in my mouth nevertheless. I tell myself it's because I went to take rather than give. (Our grannies would have said, 'God punished you!') Actually it was horrible. I don't know what I was thinking of, flying off to find something that's sitting right here under my nose. I thought I could leave my cares behind and be happy. But don't leave yourself behind; you take yourself and your emotional baggage everywhere you go. Light and darkness, pain and joy, war and peace. All of it. Lord, to myself I feel like a very heavy piece of baggage. I should be able to go off without dragging all this behind me.

Happiness lies in the giving of yourself.

I left eagerly
To return disappointed.
I thought to find new pastures, Lord,
New fruit to pick, new fruit to taste.
But the world is a deserted orchard when my hands are
closed, unable to receive.
I thought I could find some light and warmth by going
to the sun, Lord.
But the world is a dark place and the night deep when
my windows are shut.
I thought in looking at the world, Lord,
That I could find a beautiful poem to soothe my soul.
But the world is an ugly stage if I'm the actor on it.

I left eagerly
To return disappointed.
I know why, Lord,
If the world looked grey, it's because it was reflecting my
colour.

279

I feel much better after writing down my thoughts and feelings, putting a little of this life churning in me on paper.

Being able to express yourself and offer some insights — tiny canals to irrigate man's earth — is allowing man to do what he was made for: create.

People need ways to express themselves. We must teach young people a few essentials of a 'language' that will teach them to voice their feelings.

It's all very well to strum on a guitar, dance and sing, paint, whatever. But discouragement will soon set in because the basics are missing. It is important to teach children, indeed insist on, the basic principles — the 'alphabet' — even if they protest.

I'm sure somewhere there's at least one murdered Mozart, but most are still around, seriously mutilated, and can only express their feelings through violent means . . .

280

You're driving in the dark with your lights out and you complain! Turn on your lights and you'll see the road.

Lighting a dark road is in your hands. The light in you is the Lord. Welcome it, and you will walk in the light.

God is light, 'a light that shines in the dark, a light that darkness could not overpower' (John 1:5-6).

281

Man is a wonderful creature, but what a mysterious one! I will never understand him; but the more I probe, the more I discover how infinitely great he is. And the more I discover him, the more I love him.

I couldn't be a priest if I didn't love man, if I didn't try with all my strength to enter this extraordinary movement of God towards humanity. God is in love with man to the extent of becoming man himself, and turning man into a god.

The man in whom God's love does not produce love of his fellow man is living an illusion. A true meeting with God is a prelude to meeting man. It is the look of love over all creation which is the origin of the Incarnation: 'God so loved the world that he sent his only begotten son. . . .'

282

What kind of man am I? What kind of people are we? At once earth and spirit; animal and human; man and god. Bound to the dust of the earth and the stars in the sky; to the grass and the trees, the sheep and cattle. Bound to all men everywhere for all time. Living crossroads of the universe, its belly and heart daily giving birth to man.

The world and the self must be united; and I, a priest, a servant within the Church at the heart of all mankind, must help build and 'order' this world to its rightful end: men — priests of creation; myself — priest of Jesus Christ. Struggle, suffering, spilt blood; joy of success, pain of failure. Why be surprised that in me, in the world and in the Church, the work of bringing to birth should be so painful?

I will deliver myself and together we will deliver the world in pain.

283

This evening a man spent hours explaining to me that 'we' were forgetting God's transcendence by turning Christ into a chum, a pal, a buddy. The discussion was calm enough at the start, but I ended up feeling aggressive and sarcastic. Still, I tried to curb my tongue, but I thought: Here's another person who wants Jesus to walk ten feet above the ground, the same Jesus who *walked on earth like any other man*, and (just try stopping me once I get going!) had dirty feet and not even a bathroom in his house to wash in! Now why did I think that? My Jesus with dirty feet? Good heavens! I thought, reflected and prayed, a touch amused at first, but then I got more serious and wrote the following prayer for the man I had argued with earlier — and for myself.

PRAYER of the (very sincere) man who flies to the rescue of the Son of God and to the defence of 'true' religion: Lord, I 'love' you, and it's because I do that I dare speak to you this way. I kneel respectfully before you and ask your forgiveness, but I must admit I don't understand your attitude. You love mankind, but your love (forgive me) has made you lose your reason. You really didn't behave too well when you were on earth. You forgot your place, your rank. In all your meetings, talks and gestures on earth you lowered yourself and, really, that won't do. You had a position to think of as the Son of the Eternal Father, yet you lowered yourself to the level of the basest people, and you tried to lift them up to yours. One just doesn't do that. I understand that you had to be charitable and good, but you could have done that and kept your place. I also admit that you had to speak in a way that simple people could understand, but — forgive me for saying this — you didn't quite escape the risk of demagoguery. For us, your faithful, you had some very harsh words. Fortunately, we knew that it was just a way of talking and that we all say things we don't mean. But I should tell you quite frankly that you shocked a lot of us. If we've remained faithful to our religion it's because we know that in the end, it's the only thing that can maintain order in society and its morals. But we often have to fight to give you your rightful place. Many of your so-called disciples and even priests (!) seem to forget who you are. It's not surprising, Lord. You keep taking the side of the people, so the people take you for one of their own and think that all is permitted! They treat you like a chum, a pal, a buddy.

Allow me to insist, Lord. I want to be honest with you to the end. You said you were returning to your Father but you let slip carelessly that you were staying among us to the end of time. Obviously you didn't realise what you were saying, but many took you seriously, and now they see you everywhere. Some even go as far as to say that you're part of the revolution and the class struggle!

Lord, it's not true that you're always here among us and that you 'interfere' in our affairs; that you stubbornly insist on taking the side of the underdog; that you plant your 'seed of heaven' everywhere; that you're present when a collective agreement is being signed and when we're electing our deputies — is it? Your mission is over. Everything is now in place for us to receive your riches from above. All we need do is respect your commandments and humbly pray to you for grace.

You came to us 2,000 years ago. It was a great adventure, but now it's just a touching memory. A little fling, a passion, but all's back to normal now, isn't it? And if it isn't, then I beg you, Lord – in the interest of our religion – return to your rightful place. Otherwise you'll spoil everything. To be able to return again, you must depart completely.

Dear Lord, be reasonable, take your leave. Your Father, Almighty God, awaits you up there.

Lord, forgive me for what I've just written. It's easy to be flippant. But you know me. I'm not wicked; it's just that sometimes I need to let off steam. Forgive me especially for not being able to talk calmly with this man without hurting or shocking him. If he had known me better, he would have known that I too have difficulty in looking the Father in the eyes and being familiar with him, and even believing in him. God becoming man – it's so wonderful, so difficult to understand, it's annihilating! It's true we often want to put him where we want him. It's true that it's difficult to find and recognise him at work in this dense humanity, whose members tear each other apart, limb from limb. Your Father's field is full of mud, Lord. Why did you join us in it and get your feet dirty?

Lord, you could have come on an official visit to earth, to a reception with flowers and motorcycle escorts and army parades, with a couple of gorillas to protect you (bodyguards even more efficient than your own). You could have waited for the advent of television and been relayed all over the world by satellite. We could have had all your speeches recorded on tape, and the exegetes wouldn't have to argue about what you said and what you didn't. We could have had photos and films of your every word and gesture: Jesus at the United Nations; Jesus being greeted by General de Gaulle; Jesus shaking hands with Mao Tse Tung; Jesus getting out of his limousine and talking to the peasants; Jesus at prayer addressing his Father. The work of catechists would have been cut out for them, the liturgy been more alive, and priests would have little to say because you'd have been preaching at mass on Sundays (on a colour TV screen). And because this official visit would inevitably end badly – since your radical stance would stir up a lot of opposition – arrest, kangaroo court, torture and execution would have followed. There would emerge from somewhere a Joseph of Arimathea or someone from the ranks of the world media to film and record everything. While your mother, Mary, at the moment of your execution would find a way to take a last picture of you with the pocket camera John gave her on her last birthday.

Lord, you could come among us knowing how to participate in international conferences. You could have explained the creation, the infinite, the mystery of life and the depth of man. You could have saved us the trouble of having to tell the story of Adam and Eve, the serpent and the apple. You could have come as a powerful manager and solved our problems in a few words. A Superchief at the head of a Supercatholic Supersociety sweeping away all wretchedness and poverty. You could have come as a professor of sociology, economics, political science, had yourself unanimously elected secretary-general of the United Nations (well, they did want to make you their king). You could have chosen to continue your work as head of some ivy-league institution; you could have done this, you could have done that . . . if only you'd asked us, we could have told you what to do. And what we did tell you, you rejected!

Lord, you came as a stranger, secretly entering the frontiers of humanity. You stayed hidden in such an unexpected fashion. Poor, a man among men, so much a man of the people that no one noticed you. When you finally made your presence known, you turned your back on those who were attracted to you. You said and did unusual things. Even your own people thought you were crazy! Then you asked innocently: Who do people say I am? How did you expect them to recognise you?

It was inevitable that it should all end badly. Like all men who died before you and who continue dying after you, victims of the messages they carried, you were arrested, judged, tortured and executed. This was the price you paid for your unconditional solidarity with mankind, sticking with your free and crazy commitment to the bitter end. You wanted to remain a man in the eyes of men, the smallest of men, the poorest, the most despised of men. You were stripped and abandoned . . . so that we could finally come to realise that *only your love* can save the world.

Oh my Jesus of the dirty feet, looking at you on the cross, how hard it is to say to you: 'My Lord and my God! My Saviour, our Saviour!'

Now I often think about what you said — words searing my feeble heart: a disciple is not above his master!

Lord, I could never ever put myself in your position.

284

I've just re-read what I wrote the other night (above) and it occurred to me, Lord, that if it is difficult to see you — the Son of God — as the Jesus of dirty feet, it's just as difficult to see you as the resurrected Christ, living among us today. You are, as always, so discreet, invisible to our eyes. Still I believe with all my strength that you are among us, a Presence without a face, a Word without a voice, an Action without motion. We are reduced to following in your footsteps, and we still fight with one another. Some say, 'Look, he's there!' Others, 'It's a mistake, or a mirage,' and still others, 'Listen, he's talking over there!'

I'm looking for you, Lord. I want so much to meet you, for my sake and my brothers'. Armed with knowledge I search for you, but you remain hidden, elusive, as do the mysteries of your Kingdom, even from the sight of 'wise men and scholars'.

Lord, make me hear! Lord, make me see! 'But you, who do you say I am?' Then Simon Peter spoke up, 'You are the Christ, the Son of the Living God.' Jesus replied, 'Simon, son of Jonah, you are a happy man! Because it was not flesh and blood that revealed this to you but my Father in heaven' (Matthew 16:15—17).

'And their eyes were opened and they recognised him . . .' (Luke 24:31 — the disciples at Emmaus).

Lord, if I prayed more, I would know you better.

285

For many leaders of men, the ideal is not to 'direct', but to 'accompany' them on their life's journey. This is so both within the Church and the outside world. The educator accompanies his charges, the chaplain accompanies his parishioners and youth movements, the bishop accompanies his priests, episcopal committees accompany movements 'in their research' . . .

Young people, and even not-so-young people, often don't know where they're heading, so they tend to go round in circles; educators, chaplains and bishops tend to go round in circles with them. Obviously this state of affairs can't last.

Certainly, nothing should be *imposed*; rather it is a matter of *proposing*. There are silences which are called respect for others, discretion, ability to listen, but which are, in reality, *fear* — fear of asserting oneself, and especially fear of being judged negatively. A pastor must announce the Good News. It is his essential duty. As any person in charge of people, he must not pressure them or use any kind of force; he must say very clearly: 'This is where I'm going. It's a wonderful place, I invite you to accompany me.' If those travelling with him go astray, he must have the courage (and it is no easy matter) to say in a loud voice: 'I think you're making a mistake, and I'll tell you why.'

286

It is relatively easy to accept the weaknesses of a friend. It is sometimes difficult to accept his strengths.

If, however, your friend accepts your strengths and is even happy for you, then you can tell him your weaknesses without fear — for he will suffer them with you.

287

How another sees you depends on how you see him. Respect him, and he will respect you.

288

'School for Prayer'. This expression has always shocked me profoundly. I can never understand the notion that one has to 'learn' how to pray. Unless it involves some sort of physical exercise for mental relaxation, thereby to facilitate prayer . . . but that's not prayer. Prayer is given to us by God. It is his gift through the Holy Spirit. Prayer isn't 'learned'. Certainly we can be taught different approaches to prayer — that would be more honest — and some advice on how to be open to God, perhaps, but anything else is illusory.

Is there a school that teaches how to love one's parents? Do those who 'learn' how to make love, love better?

Prayer cannot be learned or taught; it is shared. If you want to get your brothers to pray, pray yourself, among them. Pray with them and they'll pray with you. But don't forget to help them live Christ's example. It's in learning to *live* that you learn to pray.

289

Prayer should not be confused with the different methods of meditation, concentration and relaxation, which are enjoying a great vogue these days. They are useful safety nets for lost Westerners who want to reunite their hearts and bodies, so dangerously abandoned. But they can't really fill that deep need which only a *meeting* with God can fill. Modern man has been relentlessly searching for 'something' for a long time; now he realises that in fact he's searching for 'someone'. Let Christians be sure and tell these seekers that they won't meet Jesus Christ through 'techniques' — they'll only meet him in the depths of their lives.

290

She's twenty years old and normally bursting with health, but she's exhausted. Lately she's been sleeping in very late and getting up feeling tired. She drags herself round from chair to chair, from armchair to armchair. She's in the grips of a mysterious tiredness.

He is known for his laziness. However, for the last three months, he's been getting up every night to work. He sleeps only a few hours. He's in love and planning to go away with the object of his affections. He's in fine form. Love has awakened in him extraordinary energies that he himself didn't think he was capable of.

Chronically exhausted people seem to be more common these days. It's not a healthy, tired feeling, the kind you get after a hard day's work or some vigorous exercise. It's more like having your breath pounded out of you, like a boxer at the losing end of a match. It's exhaustion brought on by the stress of modern living and the eternal chase after 'happiness'. Bits of your life get lost, you are physically debilitated by psychological tension; your life inevitably breaks up into little pieces.

People must again be given reasons to live, reasons good enough to motivate them into picking up the pieces, sealing up the cracks, regaining their vitality and living again.

291

When movements (I'm thinking specifically of Church movements, but this could apply equally to political and trade unionist ones for example) have existed, and been effective, for a long time, especially when they've assembled many people within their ranks and done a good job, they tend to harden into all-too-perfect casts. Such movements want to shape people in these casts, and are surprised that few are willing to let themselves be moulded. They forget that, by definition, a movement is mobile, that the world and its occupants progress and evolve, nothing stands still, and that their so-called loyalty to their movement is just a temporary fixation. But good casts, which have produced great shapes, are difficult to break ... and it's even harder to fashion new ones, based on yesterday's experience, for today's man in today's world.

292

I'm afraid those two may desire rather than love each other. (A young couple just came to ask about having a Church wedding.) I tried to explain, in simple terms, that love isn't something to be plucked and eaten for mutual pleasure — that's just a momentary alliance of two selfish beings. It's *giving* yourself freely to the other, on all levels, and receiving each other in a new, mutually enriching life.

Loving is helping the other to exist. It's giving him or her life before uniting to create a third life, a child. Desire is a sign, a departure point, which sets man on the road to woman, and woman to man, but love surpasses desire. Whoever stops at desire will never know how to love. Desire is a force, not a goal — it helps you to love, but it isn't love. Sometimes you have to love without desire. Love then

becomes *wanting*. It's difficult. So many people think: 'We
don't love each other any more.' That means they've never
loved each other, just desired each other. When they've
taken all they can from the other, they look elsewhere for
another desire, another fulfilment.

There are lovers who should be saying to each other:
'I desire you so much that I've no strength to love.' Because
that's exactly what they're doing.

293

Loving is an exciting but difficult adventure. It requires
much effort to transform it from desire to a *desire to give*.
This is true of all human love, but even more so of God's
love.

Whoever dedicates his life to God is, like any man, a
man of desires, but only one desire surfaces, and all other
desires are centred on it without disturbing anything. Drawn
to Jesus Christ, he often begins by attempting to 'meet' him;
he will soon understand though that it's more a matter of
giving himself to Christ and welcoming him, very often in the
night — the night of the 'senses' and the spirit, which mystics
talk about. God is not taken; he is given.

There's no such thing as many kinds of love.

Lord, if I didn't search for you to 'take' you, perhaps
you wouldn't hide from me so much.

294

Why are you so much on my mind these days, Jacques?
I've known you for a long time. You come into my mind,
along with so many others and stubbornly sit there on my
brain, bringing back memories, making me think. You
make me realise that I have no right to avoid myself —
I so often want to escape far from my daily life and go
and 'flirt' with God in some peaceful place (when I say
'flirt', I mean joining God for the 'spiritual' pleasure that
he sometimes gives me). To be always ready and available
to one and all is a difficult thing. So many people come
through my life! I remember the stranger who entered
France illegally, having escaped from a displaced persons'

camp in Central Europe after the Second World War. I never knew exactly who he was. I wonder if he himself knew. He was twenty years old and laden with as many years' worth of suffering. He had been wandering about, homeless, hungry, without work, or love, for weeks when I met him in Paris. I think I gave him all I could – nourishment and friendship. He was so ravenously hungry!

I tried to help him get work. He needed a permit, but to get the permit, he had to have a job. It was a vicious circle. I asked some friends of mine to take him in; I took him to see some people in organisations for aid to foreigners and did what I could before leaving. I had to go, and before I left, I gave him my address. I didn't expect him to write (he could barely speak French) but I didn't want to lose touch with him. I wanted to tell him: 'Jacques, this is what I'm here for, I'm here for you, you have all my affection, my dear unknown brother.'

Two weeks later he was on my doorstep. He had found me in my tiny village in Normandy where I was working at the time. To get to me, he'd stolen a bicycle and cycled for four or five hours. He was exhausted, but spoke of returning very shortly as he had to report daily to the authorities where he was living. He was afraid of being late getting back. He asked for nothing and, I admit, I wondered why he'd come at all. He seemed so anxious to get back. So I walked with him on the road and presently I was the one who was saying 'You'd better hurry or you'll be late.' And he said, 'Walk a little longer with me.' We walked. And I kept thinking: Why have you come?

The moment came to say goodbye. I nervously fingered a banknote I wanted to give him. I was afraid of offending him, so I tried to slip it into his pocket. But he saw me and leaped back protesting. I didn't think he would accept it, yet I insisted clumsily, 'Buy yourself a beer on the way back.' Nothing doing. So I said reproachfully, 'Why not, Jacques, aren't we brothers?' And he replied, looking me straight in the eye, 'If I took it you might think that's what I came for. All I wanted was to see you.' Then lowering his eyes and blushing slightly, he added: 'I wanted you to embrace me.'

I embraced him and he left.

The road was straight. I stayed there for a long time watching him cycle away in the distance. I could see him for miles. He kept turning around and waving.

This was a few days before Christmas. About five days later, I received a note from the supervisor of the hostel Jacques was living in. Jacques had committed suicide on Christmas Eve. They had found my address on his bedside table; above my name he had written, 'Notify my brother.' The supervisor's note also said, 'He told us a lot about you, he loved you very much.'

I know why I'm thinking about you tonight, Jacques. It's because of the meeting I was just at, where I tried to get through to some devout and sincere Christian women that charity doesn't consist in merely helping your neighbour in need through a few small gestures, even if these gestures are at times essential. It consists also in fighting, each from his own corner but united in groups and organisations, to change the world's structures and to guide and direct the movements of history which mangle people before killing them off.

Jacques, it was the war, deportations, camps, rules and regulations that killed you. You didn't kill yourself. I know that much.

Yet so many Christians fail to grasp the true 'dimension of charity' as Father Lebret used to say. However, at the other end of the scale, there are those who believe a just and peaceful society could never exist without the 'embrace of a brother'.

295

A vague feeling of anguish is prowling around in me like a caged beast, immobilising my energies and concentration. The feeling has no shape and I don't know what to call it. I am its prisoner. I've got to shake it off. I need all my energy at the moment, at every moment, if I'm to live my life in its fullness. But I won't be free of it until I've let the bad feeling wash over me, then faced it without fear, grabbed it with both hands and offered it to God who can bring new life even out of sin.

I can understand the awful pain of those who are suffering

from depression. It's a paralysing of one's whole being, while others whisper: He should pull up his socks! Control himself! But the trouble is *he can't*. It's an ordeal, one of the worst. He needs drugs, perhaps. But he also needs someone always to be there, patient, sensitive, to help him set free the little pieces of life which are stagnating in him, polluting his source. And if he is a believer, he must also be helped to offer it all to God.

296

There is no 'forbidden' love. It's never bad to really and truly love. It is bad, however, to love badly. But loving at times means distancing yourself, leaving, to allow the 'other' freedom to give himself, and receive another.

297

A priest, like any man, must love and build his 'unity'. If he doesn't love, he amputates part of himself. No one can live without loving. He hasn't married a woman, but he must marry nevertheless . . . it's not good for man to be alone. A priest does not refuse to marry, he marries at another level — 'God', people say. It's not really 'satisfying', if I may put it that way. Attracted by Jesus Christ, he attempts to welcome him and give himself to him, but by 'marrying' Jesus Christ, through Him and in Him, he marries the whole of humanity.

Love Jesus Christ, love him in all mankind, otherwise you'll always be a cripple.

298

A church association has reaffirmed its distaste for 'propaganda and proselytisation' and its wish to 'bear witness to the resurrected Christ in daily life' quietly, and always ready to listen. This is no doubt an admirable attitude — certainly a serious and valid one — but it demands that we be perfect — that is, that our lives *be* the Gospel, the Good News, presented to modern man and *readable by all*.

Personally, I know full well that my life doesn't mirror Jesus Christ that well, but I refuse to shut up. I will continue to say what I believe. I will also say that I don't always practise all the things I passionately believe. And I'm not the only one, alas. I will add that I can only try; all we sinners can but try to live together as best we can.

Somewhere between the noise and the silence is room for a true, if humble, word. One must have the courage to speak up!

299

Children of my heart, you're getting married tomorrow and I will be blessing your union. You will say: X. will you be my wife? (Yes, I give myself to you.) And you, X., will say: Will you be my husband? (Yes, I give myself to you.) And together, silently, you will ask Jesus Christ: Will you commit yourself with us? And Christ will whisper in your hearts: Yes, I give myself to you. But do you give yourselves to me? Are you willing to bear witness to my love among your brothers?

If you accept, then you will answer Yes, and you will give infinite love a recognisable *face*. And I, I'll never tire of watching you smile, laugh and dance all night. I'll see Christ's love in your joy.

300

If the other walks all over you deliberately, don't send him packing. It's a sign that he needs you. He's reminding you he's there. That's all. Listen to him; welcome him; recognise him . . . even if you think you really know him.

301

Being proud is not recognising your gifts and talents, it's being stupid enough to think you've got gifts you don't possess, and forgetting that the ones you do have, have been given to you gratuitously.

302

Tell the ones you love that you love them.
 'But they know it already!'

Perhaps, but they need to hear you say it . . . and *believe* it. You can't live not knowing or believing that you're loved.

303

(In Brazil, visiting French volunteer priests to the Latin American aid programme)

I want to record and remember the following because it helped me understand to what extent the Brazilians — the little people, the poor of the nation, that is — could be marked in their collective memory by the slavery which they've suffered. If today their masters have changed their image, the slaves remain. The people must be freed.

Marcel, a French priest, said to me: 'The other day, a Black kid told me in confession that he'd run away from his father who'd been beating him. Can you imagine? He thought that running away from the beating was a sin. He's not the only kid who thinks like that. Back in the last century, when a slave was punished, he was whipped. If he ran away, he was caught and beaten even more. It was the master's right to punish, and the slave's duty to accept that punishment.'

Flesh gets scarred, but so does the soul. The scars are hidden. From generation to generation, the poor have continued to submit to their masters and even . . . to God,. the Almighty Master: 'God willed it,' they repeat when they're suffering. That was their catechism — allowing themselves to be 'whipped' by God.

We must get men off their knees and break their chains. We must heal their souls, dress their wounds, wipe out the humiliation they've suffered and give them back their dignity. We must tell them that they are as much the sons of God as their masters.

Some say that this is creating subversion. Absolutely not! Rather, it's creating upright men, worthy of their Father 'who is in heaven'.

304

This afternoon, during a conversation with Dom Helder Camara, I suddenly switched off. I no longer heard what he was saying; I was staring at him, mesmerised.

I'm not the first to be overwhelmed by this man. On this particular occasion, he seemed tinier than ever, his body shrinking but his face growing – in particular, his eyes, mouth and ears – all his facial 'orifices', what morpho-psychologists would term the vestibules – while his arms, hands and legs seemed to be in a state of ceaseless change. As usual, he gesticulated, punctuating every word, every sentence, his hands and arms flying, soaring like an eagle in flight.

Dom Helder is physically quite small, but his capacity to contain and accommodate all the poor of the earth is staggering. His small frame fills a huge space. He's a giant! How did he attain such a dimension? Confined to his office, he is present as much in his beloved north-eastern Brazil as he is in North America and Europe. His voice reaches every corner of the earth. He gives confidence to millions of poor people. He uplifts them. He worries the rich and powerful.

I had come to discuss the French priests in his diocese. When I asked him what kind of work they were doing for his diocese, he immediately interrupted me – never mind the work, he wanted to speak of *them* first. How did you find them? How are they? Are they happy? He was interested in each and every one of those priests, he was concerned about them individually, he wanted to know what he, Dom Helder, could do for them.

We eventually got around to the subject of the French priests' work. We talked for a long time, because for every observation I made, he gave me long explanations, describing the people, their poverty and suffering, their aspirations. He told me how, nourished by the Scriptures, changed from within men united and lived together, not only to combat injustice, but also to pray and celebrate together. I could see these 'basic communities' which we hear about in France, but which actually exist here, take shape before my very eyes.

When I was ready to leave, he stopped me, still talking. He hadn't quite finished. He asked me to come back and gave me a long final embrace (a true Brazilian *abracao*, a mutual embrace with lots of hearty pats on the back). He seemed to be saying, 'I'm taking you with me. I'm keeping

177

you with me.' And it was true. Every time I see Dom Helder, even if it's been a while between meetings, I'm always deeply touched by his questions and concern. He seems to know my affairs better than I do. I could never fathom out how he could be so intensely present, remembering individuals and their interests, as well as in a general sense. But we know his secret now — since his early days at the seminary, he's been getting up in the night to meditate and pray. He welcomes the world and his God into his large open heart. Every night, this tiny man grows a little more!

305

(thinking of Dom Helder)

Violence for violence's sake is destructive. Only the violence of love can accomplish anything.

He says: 'To use violence without love is like trying to put out a fire with a blazing torch.'

306

When I was barely eighteen and showing the first signs of discovering the Lord and wanting to enter the seminary, I could sum it all up in a few words: loving and giving yourself. It was a sort of device, and I was quite proud of it. It seemed to describe exactly what I wanted to do with my life.

Not long ago I realised that when I was looking for a title to Danny's diary, the first word that came to mind was 'loving'. Later on, for Anne-Marie's diary, I thought of 'giving yourself' (I subsequently dropped the 'yourself' to avoid any ambiguity). Loving, giving oneself — this was twelve years after I had first thought of these words.

I read somewhere that we think of two or three original ideas in our lifetime. That's all. The more gifted among us maybe get four or five. And I believe it. I also believe that we each have to live one or two words of the Gospel, those which the Spirit has mysteriously spoken to all of us.

Loving, giving oneself. I think that these are Christ's words to me, boundless words which I haven't finished exploring, and which I have put into practice much too little — so much so that I would be afraid to appear before God if I didn't believe with all my strength that God is love.

307

Man has set up camp in a tiny little corner of himself. From time to time, he ventures out of his tent to fetch some water from a stream close by. But he never goes beyond the boundaries of his camp grounds.

Man is undiscovered territory.

308

On the long drive back this evening, I tried to pray but couldn't stay with it. So I stopped trying and started looking at the countryside around me.

The road was magnificent on this late autumn day. The rays of the setting sun burnished everything in sight. I felt like a king driving up his private road to his palace. The branches of the trees, silhouetted against the sky like a wild gypsy's hair spread on a pillow of light, fascinated me. On I drove between these ghostly faces and their dark secrets.

I felt very limited, powerless, unable to detach myself from the earth and reach for heaven. Tonight, in my mouth, my eyes and my heart, there is a bitter taste of paradise lost.

309

Once again I'm alone this evening, and as I pause from my work the chill wind of loneliness sweeps into the room. I don't need words; quite the contrary, I need silence. I don't need to be caressed; physically, I feel fine. My need goes much deeper. I need a silent and loving presence — someone to be there, if not for me, then with me.

I know you're there, Lord — but I know it intellectually, not physically. What can I do with a presence that is absent physically?

If I could only have a 'sixth sense' to touch you with!

Lord, why do you hide yourself?

I know your answer, but it's addressed to my head — tonight my heart and my flesh are asking the question.

310

I remember a night I spent in hospital a long time ago. I couldn't sleep because of an awful whimpering that pierced the heavy silence. I searched in the dark for the source of that suffering. It was a child, a tiny little child. Later I learned that it had been badly burned.

I whispered a few words to it and caressed its damp forehead with one hand, while with the other I held up the sheet — the contact with the child's burning flesh must have been painful. The whimpering stopped. But when I finally crept away, it started up worse than before. I couldn't bear it, so I went back. I don't remember how long I stayed by the child's side.

That episode made me realise more than ever that when there's nothing left to use against pain, love is the only answer — love in the form of total presence of body, mind and spirit, wide open and supportive. The pain is still there but the victim no longer has to bear it alone.

At the foot of the cross, Mary carried her son's pain in the same way.

311

Only a liberator can be a free man.

312

(notes from a retreat)
I can meet God in the depths of my being, my real self. It's true. That's where he is, that's where he moves, that's where the source springs forth. I must go beyond my different faces — they're just a screen, in the way.

I'm thirsty. I'm invited to drink. I hear the call, the voice, but I have difficulty finding the way to the source. First, I must allow silence to enter me, then I must listen. Don't force it.

I'm always surprised to find it so near. It's the path on the other side of the bush, but I don't see it. I imagine it's miles away. I'm dying of thirst not knowing that the source is right there. It's madness!

I wanted to look at the countryside; instead I was invited to go indoors. I shut my eyes, and immediately I saw that He was infinitely more beautiful than any countryside.

Experiencing God. An indescribable embrace, dazzling, breath-taking. A certainty, a sureness that wipes out months and years of searching, thinking, doubts and discussion. Oh yes, you can reason on the subject of God, but 'knowing' him (being born to him) is a different matter altogether!

I need to write down these moments of life — real life, not the superficial daily spectacle that passes for life. I'm trembling. I fear that words may turn out to be obstacles.

A few minutes, and I'm drunk with light. I don't know anything any more. I just feel very peaceful.

I'm happy. I daren't think of anything else — I'm afraid it might all vanish into thin air. Lord, I know I've no right to flirt with you. I know that I've been absent too long from you and that you want me back. But you'll only hide from me again, just like the sun which I adore. Why? I need sunshine.

313

There is a place where God speaks to you and it's closer than you think — it is in *you*. Stop for a moment, close your eyes and keep quiet. You've arrived. Now listen.

Your Lord has just said: 'If anyone loves me he will keep my word, and my father will love him, and we shall come to him *and make our home with him*' (John 14:23).

'But I'm not practising God's Word.'

'You're trying though, aren't you.'

'Yes.'

'Then "they" are there — the Lord said nothing about only loving saints.'

314

For months, even years, all X. has been able to say in answer to her psychotherapist's questions and mine, is a barely audible 'I don't know.' Then she retires into her silence — a heavy silence that's more like a prison wall. No one can enter.

The other day I tried again to reach her. And again she murmured, 'I don't know.' 'Oh yes, you do!' I snapped impatiently.

Today I received a painful, sensitive letter from her. She explained: 'That's all I can say — no other words will come out. I have to keep saying it; it's my way of keeping the door open and not blocking myself forever.'

I regretted having snapped at her.

Unfortunately X. isn't the only 'prisoner' I know. These unhappy people remain closed, mute, strangled, harbouring a turbulence they can never express. They are slowly dying because they can't connect to other people. We shall never know the extent of their suffering; they are like people buried alive.

The Gospel says that Jesus cured a lot of mutes. What can I do to help my brothers speak again?

315

You're discouraged because somewhere in your life, or in the life of others, love has failed. If you want to recover, you must try offering a loving gesture. It will put you back on the road to hope, and life. For a failed love is death, and love itself is life.

316

You can buy yourself a rock
You can be offered a rock
You can crash against a rock
Rocks can be thrown at you.
If you're standing upright, you can take all these rocks wherever they come from and build a wall for your house.

317

Sin is always the result of broken bonds — man's desire to ravish and 'capitalise' on life (people and objects), and to cling to it all, refusing to pass anything on.

Sin not only shatters man's bonds with God but also with others. It shatters all humanity.

318

Only Christ can reunite humanity and reconstitute the 'total body'. That's what he came for — to bring God's dispersed children together so they can have life and have it in abundance.

By becoming flesh — a man — Jesus reunited humanity. Perfection itself, he excluded no one from his communion. He is on our side, to the end; he receives and carries us lovingly, refusing no one. We become 'incorporated' in him, his death and his resurrection. In him all mankind now has *life*.

319

Christians are people who recognise Christ as being the Man/ Son of God, and by welcoming him, they receive 'abundant life', 'eternal life'. Together they consciously become the Body of Christ, that is, the Church. In this context Christ isn't complete. As St Paul put it, he hasn't reached his adult height yet.

320

Accept your life as it is — but exclude sin. Don't dream of another life, otherwise you'll endanger your present one. You'll jeopardise your 'cohabitation' with your actual life, and if you sleep in different rooms you'll never procreate. In your honeymoon with your daily life Christ awaits you. He has a new life for you, one which will never end.

321

You often try to run away from your life, but you're wasting your time.

If you sincerely believe that your life is worthwhile and necessary, then you will have accepted it.

322

You musn't just tolerate yourself. You must also *love* yourself. If you don't love yourself, how could you possibly love your brother? The Lord asks you to love him as yourself.

Loving yourself means first accepting your limitations and weaknesses. Then, *believing in yourself*, that is, being confident in the knowledge that the Lord has given you all you need to do what you must do, wherever you find yourself.

323

I've just been shown around a section of a large provincial town, which is in the process of being renovated. People have fought to get something done about the slums, and poverty, in these parts. They've agitated, signed petitions, discussed solutions and made it all happen. It's very good and it was necessary — but it's not enough.

Some looked beyond the renovation and said: 'We must also educate (or re-educate) the people.' Teams of social workers and educators set about re-educating attitudes and mentalities. It's still not enough.

Education isn't everything, especially when it concerns those who haven't really thought about it or had to fight for it, and it can't teach people how to respect buildings and neighbourhoods. They must also be taught to *love*. This is a much much harder thing to teach. Who's going to do it? In fact, who's even going to dare suggest that it needs doing?

I didn't say anything.

324

Man exists within relationships — not with individuals, but individuals who themselves exist within relationships. Thus, he is a *being in society*. He participates in a society made up of all sorts of different characters. From them he receives life as he gives it. Sometimes he has to defend himself against it. He is influenced; he is transformed. He in turn influences and transforms others. People assemble naturally (which is why they tend to stick together) on several, overlapping, levels:

Biological   (race)
Social   (social class, i.e. working, upper, etc.)
Geographical (country, town, district, apartment building, etc.)

| Functional | (profession, leisure, studies, etc.) |
| Action | (movements, associations, organisations, etc.) |

You can't 'reduce' man to just one of the above. At best, it would only belittle him; at worst, it would deform and turn him into a monster. For each individual, you need to look for his main characteristics while trying to pinpoint the ones that predominate at the moment, for they are not fixed things. Life evolves, progresses and changes daily.

325

What we call 'normality' is never neutral. Customs and habits are always vehicles of sin or love. That being the case, they set man on the path either to regression or to moral progress.

326

You can attempt to separate quarrelling children; you can judge them, and tell one he's wrong, and the other he's right; or you can decide not to intervene at all. In any case you're taking a stand, because even deciding against intervention is taking a stand.

Thus, people who claim that they're non-political are mistaken. Political neutrality is in itself a political position. Everyone has a political position.

327

The aim of politics is to put certain structures in place to ensure that respect for man, his development, responsibilities and freedom can grow in an environment of justice and peace. His final aim should be to create a world in which it would be possible to love without having to be a hero. But this love can never be released by a politician — he simply doesn't have the key.

328

Once men have been rushed off by their leaders to fight gigantic and complex wars and get wounded, frightened and exhausted, they will return home with a well-founded reluctance ever to leave again.

329

Before training men to deal with the roots of bloodshed — poverty, injustice and slavery and so on — they must be taught what to do about its bitter fruit, the suffering that results from warfare.

From that point they can realise gradually that they must attack the causes of war and their commitment will be the stronger for having been born out of bitter first-hand experience.

330

Just as it was thought that developing science and technology would bring happiness and progress, there are people today who think that building just, social, economic and political structures will bring happiness and progress.

It is true that better conditions help, but it's illusory to believe that they alone are sufficient. Man doesn't change, and structures in themselves don't radically change anything — unless *man himself takes part in these changes* for himself and his brothers. What changes him then is his commitment, his dedication to others. It becomes a spiritual mission at the core of which the believer recognises the presence of God.

331

Mrs X., who has been paralysed for years now, told me the other day that her paralysis was bothering her more than usual. Her friends and neighbours are insensitive at times and discuss their vacations with her. They tell her they need a rest, a change of air and relaxation . . . as she sits there unable to move. I tried to explain to her that she musn't 'resign' herself to it — it's so unfair that she should be paralysed. All suffering is bad. Her duty is to fight it; she has the right to cry, to shout. But I also pointed out that she musn't let it all go to waste; she must offer it up to Jesus Christ. All offered sufferings can produce life. I sent her the prayer below (commissioned by a religious journal in 1973). She wrote back saying: 'I tried to do what you suggested. I received post-cards from my vacationing friends and when they returned, they came and told me all about it. Do you know, for the first time, I felt really happy to see them looking so well. My vacation this year consisted of discovering that my pain can perhaps be put to some use . . .'

PRAYER for the sick, the aged and those who don't take vacations.

My pain is in my hands,
I am ill.
I carry the heavy burden of my years,
I am old.
I consume my long grey days without appetite.
I am weakened by habit,
perspiring in my overheated bed,
motionless in my chair, looking forever out of my window,
submissive in the arms of my day.
Time passes me by, with me unable to walk with it.
And yet, Lord, you invite me to this re-creation.
I must create my vacations,
  with a book to read, a few friends to receive and love,
  contact with you — the most real, the most profound.
Above all, Lord, I must, at the end of winter
put down the burden and lassitude of my years.
For long I have borne them alone, crushed
near you who wait for me . . . to help me bear them.
I will finally be able to stand up, freed, available.
I will look at others, the ones I know and the ones I don't.
And I will welcome their joy and join in their happiness.
I will take my vacation through them.
Oh, yes Lord, I will then be content,
and happy for their happiness.

332

Not for the first time, an anguished father said to me: 'I stumbled across some pornographic magazines in my son's room. What can I do?' The question came too late; he had already tackled his son about it and 'made him feel ashamed'.

I said: 'Nothing is more beautiful than the awakening of a young body and the force which projects it towards the body of another person, even if, at the beginning, it is only to satisfy new and overwhelming desires. His flesh is awakening to the yearning and loneliness of the human heart. It is an ancient and inevitable reminder that we shall find our fulfilment in a loving union; an invitation to partake of the fullness of living without which no one can be fully alive; it is life that he is experiencing and the urge to form new life. Yes, tell him how beautiful the bodies of men and women are. Tell him not to be afraid or ashamed. Little by little, from the depths of his overwhelming, sometimes obsessive, desires, a new goal will emerge. It will come from the heart, not just the flesh, and this new desire will push him into a fresh awareness that God always moves to unify our divided desires, one body and one heart in one person. Then he will be able to meet another person who has reached a similar state of maturity. Together they will engender life and, in God's image, form a trinity.

'Tell him finally that it's such a beautiful experience that he must prepare for it, that's it's also very difficult, and that you know because you've been through it.'

333

Learning how to love is learning how to give rather than take; it is enriching yourself so as to be able to enrich others. In the end it is to increasingly welcome the One who is Love itself.

334

The physical aspect of love does not in itself carry any significance. It can be a communion or a separation: a wonderful communion, if it is mutual; a tragic separation, if it is just a way of taking from each other to fulfil personal desires. In the first case, it is a meeting of two people. In the second, it is a collison of two objects.

335

Don't suppress your natural desires expecting to experience some great triumph of the spirit. However, a life devoted exclusively to sensuality can only be sterile. Your heart and body must grow together; otherwise you may be an angel or an animal, but you'll never be a man.

336

A gaping void exists in man that nothing can fill. If he decides to live in truth, going from hunger to hunger, from thirst to thirst, one day he will reach a sunny glade where life awaits him — and his emptiness will be filled. But he must first experience several deaths. He must not sit idly on the side of the road, or lose his direction on dead-end roads.

Often, when I'm talking with people who tell me about their problems, I feel that they're unconsciously looking for some sort of fulfilment or nourishment beyond what they're struggling for. I say nothing; whether it is through respect, timidity or lack of faith, I don't know. I should probably speak up, for I am a disciple of Christ, who said that he came to give us life and give it to us in abundance. Since no one else will remind them of this, perhaps I should.

337

A child's first words come from his mother. The as yet untapped richness in a child needs to be expressed, and it is his mother who teaches him how to do this.

Look upon Jesus Christ. His Spirit will offer you the words to pray, and your life, so often buried deep, will burst forth.

338

(in Rome, at a meeting of the general council of the pontifical mission on Latin America)

I've been here for three days, in this magnificent, majestic room in the Vatican, a room whose luxury shocked me at first. I wasn't expecting such sumptuousness. It clashed badly with my dreams of poverty and simplicity, as well as the idea that perhaps my simple office at home was too comfortable.

I said not a word — ten, fifteen years ago I would have exploded! Perhaps I'm wiser now. By this third day, I'm perfectly at ease in all this magnificence. One gets used to things so very quickly!

Yet, the other day, I had been thinking intensely about my priest friends in Latin America. I thought of Pierre, among others, whom I had seen in Chile barely a month before in his makeshift home — a hut without running water or electricity, the bed a piece of wood that could be put away during the day to make room, the water coming from a hole outside the hut. Pierre, I was tempted to tell you that it was a bit crazy, that you wouldn't last long in such conditions . . . but you were so happy, glowing, even though you spoke of 'shattered illusions'. You told me how happy these people were to see you settle among them — a priest living just like them. But you also told me about the woman who watched you quietly as you put up your hut — admiringly you thought — and who suddenly exclaimed: 'How rich you are Father, you've got new wood.' She and her people had only old wood for their sagging shanties. I guess you could never be quite as poor as the poor.

Pierre, I said nothing to you. I left envying you. If only you knew how much. But I don't know if I would have had your courage.

Today I'm sitting in the Vatican which, it is thought, is bulging with wealth. I know that isn't true, I know that it is one and the same Church — here dressed in luxurious finery, there dressed in tattered rags. I know, because I've been inside. A prelate of the Curia invited me up to his rooms, a tiny apartment with a magnificent view over St Peter's Square, but simpler than even the most humble village priest's dwelling. He has a car that is falling to pieces and barely gets him to the Rome suburb he ministers to every Sunday. He doesn't have the funds to buy a new one. I also know that a large hall had to be built to receive the pilgrims who come to Rome to see the Pope; that you can't raze the Vatican to the ground and in its place build a large, functional highrise, preferably in the suburbs . . . it would cost a fortune! I also know that it would be folly to break up the

Vatican museum; it is a historical heritage as valid as . . . the Kremlin. And if I'm aware of all this, I'm also aware of all the wretchedness and poverty in the world, and we must make sure that everyone else is aware of it too. The question is how.

339

There are times when I feel like a child loth to go out and play because he's studying for an exam, and nothing else matters.

But there are other times (though it doesn't happen often) when I'm at 'play' with the Lord, the bell rings for classes, and I don't want to go back in.

When will I understand that there is a time for work and a time for recreation ('re-creation'), that each is necessary, that you Lord are ever present, and, especially, that I must not give in to the desire of the moment.

340

I'm not a night person. I'm at my best in the morning. I'd like to be able to get up with the sun, pray in the silence and welcome the day's first light. Every dawn I'd like to ask the Holy Spirit to enter me and plant its seeds into the virgin day that I am about to embrace. But I'm obliged to follow the dissonant rhythm of men rushing around, always short of time, using up more and more of their nights . . . with bright neon lights they attempt to turn night into day, while they bury their days and turn them into night.

Man is 'denaturing' himself. He is a day-time bird changing into a night one.

341

When the Church begins to spend too much time counting working hours, raises in salaries, holidays and so on, it is a sign that it is becoming a business, and straying from its role as the representative of Jesus Christ in the service of his brothers.

342

The material demands of certain priests amaze and sometimes shock me. I'm told that one is only human, that the
world changes, and people today have different needs, ones
they didn't have before. The same goes for certain seminarians.
They make demands, they want to be reassured of tomorrow.

I myself have had to struggle (and I still do), bitterly at
times, against getting too settled and comfortable. Today,
more than at any other time, the temptations of general 'comfort' is difficult to resist. But Christ's invitation is always the
same: forsake your possessions and follow me. I will give
you . . . the cross!

That's all I'm going to say to anyone thinking of entering
the Church. If they want more, I shall tell them not to
bother. My only fear is that they'll find some bishop somewhere who'll encourage them nevertheless, and invite them
to come and discuss it to see what can be done . . .

343

Since I've been in charge of the vocational services of the
diocese, I'm often asked why it is, in my opinion, that so
few young people want to enter the religious life. A discussion
will ensue and inevitably there will be adults attacking the
young: they're more selfish these days, all they can think
about is their cars, their parties, their pleasure, they don't
want to risk anything, they don't want commitments, and so
on and so forth. Every time the subject comes up, I get
indignant.

Yesterday, during a question and answer period after a
lecture, the subject of vocations came up, but we were
running out of time, so I took note of all the questions and
said: 'I don't have enough time to answer you all, but I'll
tell you this much — and perhaps your questions will
be answered.

'First, you say that young people today don't want to
commit themselves. They are your children, your sons. We
adults have created the environment in which they were raised.

'Secondly, the reasons they hesitate or refuse to commit
their lives are exactly the reasons for which we all hesitate or

refuse to commit our lives, right here in society and the Church.

'Let us take a good look at ourselves. We might find the answers, in doing so, right there.'

344

What distinguishes the Christian from the non-Christian? NOTHING. The Christian is no better or worse; he is no more virtuous than the others — in fact, he might even be less so. No more loving, giving or fraternal than anyone else — there are people who love more. There's only one difference: the Christian believes God loves him and that if he welcomes this love, it will be transmitted to the world through him, and on this love the world will be built.

345

I played with a child who laughed a lot. I laughed along with him. Together, affectionately, we were at peace.

I wondered why we are so disarmed by the sight of a smiling child. I decided it's because our defences are down.

People with power scare us. We're afraid they might use their power against us, so we think about being more powerful than them, well armed, just in case.

A child inspires love; disarmed as we are before it, our hands and hearts are free to reach out and love it.

If only we could all be like little children . . .

346

How do you measure fidelity? Why do we get so discouraged at times? After all, who among us can truthfully say that he's totally faithful — in his marriage, in his commitment to the Church? The severance of bonds is not an uncommon occurrence. Our lives are a mixture of faithfulness and betrayal — small or large, public or private. It's all part of life and we shouldn't feel too disappointed with ourselves and others. Rather we should humbly accept our limitations and our sins. Only God is *faithful*. Our fidelity lies in the *will* to be faithful amid all our infidelities.

347

(after a meeting at the Vatican)

I really think I'm an incorrigible joker at times. The more serious people are, the more I'm tempted to clown around. I'm not overly fond of people who take themselves — or even serious matter — too seriously. . . .

Anyway, from the start of the meeting, Cardinal X. had insisted on addressing me as Monsignor. He just couldn't understand that I didn't have a title, especially as I was present at such a high-level meeting. During the coffee break I said to him: 'Father [that was brave of me!] I'm not a Monsignor!'

'Then you must be a canon?' he asked

'No I am not a canon, either,' I replied.

'Then, my friend, how is one to address you?' he said.

'Why not just call me Michel like everyone else?' I said, 'It is my Christian name!'

A moment's hesitation (should he or shouldn't he?) and, like a good sport, he smiled and said, 'Okay, *Michel*, what would you like, coffee or fruit juice?'

Back at the meeting, we exchanged a few ideas and the Cardinal began to ask us questions. When it was my turn, he gave me a little conspiratorial smile and, without losing an inch of his majestic dignity — but with the air of superiority of an older brother dealing with his kid brother (!) — he said, 'And you, *Michel*, what do you think?'

I confess I babbled a bit, embarrassed suddenly by the raised eyebrows of those around me and because I hadn't really been listening. My mind had been on other things . . . on how twenty years ago we'd launched a 'first-name campaign' in schools and colleges, and now I'd done it in the Vatican!

Oh, it's not serious, really. And I'm not a serious type! If I had my choice, I'd be a jester rather than a king.

348

I've just reread some of my notes (something I rarely do). I wrote following my Brazilian 'enlightenment' (No. 25) because I was so deeply moved. I collected my thoughts in the silence and placed myself, a tiny speck, in the immense humanity of today, yesterday and even tomorrow, in the centre of this billion-year-old universe. I measured my smallness — but also my greatness. I possess a wonderful ability to realise that I have bonds with this universe and mankind. I can relate to them very well; completely accepting, but also giving. I don't ever want to keep anything locked up in me; I want to pass it on, personalised, humanised. Then, carrying the greatness of man and all things, enriched by the freedom no one can ever take away from me, I can turn to you, my God, and say 'Yes' once more — the 'Yes' that Mary spoke — for our eternal happiness.

I welcome you in Jesus. I want your life to take root in me, in my heart, in one flesh. I want this life to pass through me to my brothers. I am in communion with them, for better or worse, however small my role in history, every time I say 'yes' I can nourish the whole world with you.

349

GOD IS LOVE (St John). Love was made flesh, through Mary, in Jesus of Nazareth.

Each one of us, every day, in our individual situations, in all our actions, with our brothers, must continue the process of the 'incarnation of love' throughout history so that, at the end of time, Christ will have reached his 'adult height' (see St Paul). The Church is the developing body of Christ.

350

I now realise that what I discovered in Brazil I had already discovered in life.

I had at one time conducted a study on a section of the city of Rouen (in France), one I had attacked incisively like a doctor examining a patient. It was a scientific study, but also a spiritual one for me. In all the research I conducted, I met Jesus Christ. Enriched by my experiences, I went through towns and cities, always searching for the one who said he would live among us to the end of time.

One particular day, I was waiting for a priest called Michel to discuss the JOC with him. I was in his office gazing out of the window at the roofs of the city. I looked, and prayed, for a long time (Michel was always late), then I sat at his desk and wrote, 'Lord, I want to rise to the highest peak.' I had seen Christ living in the heart of the city.

I had the same 'revelation' on a completely different occasion, in a totally different setting, when I was in Brazil. A vision of the mystery of the Love of the Father continuing through time; a certitude that everything in life, good or evil, works towards the creation of the Kingdom. In me, an almost haunting impatience to go beyond mankind, events and things, to find a *meaning* to life, all life, an answer to that burning question in my mind since before entering the seminary: what is the purpose of living if my joy and struggles and suffering, even the most insignificant, serve nothing? If life is indeed meaningless, why are we here?

Lord, I've heard it all before. I am constantly discovering what I know already; I'm walking down roads I have already travelled on. Is my vision clouded? Do I have a case of recurring blindness? Lord, cure me. I want to SEE you.

351

Perhaps some day science can explain the world (?), but it can never explain its meaning.

352

Praying surely means placing yourself naked before God, for a few moments joining in spirit all those praying all over the world, communing in the great body of Christ.

True Christian prayer involves man praying in unison with his brothers, suffused with all the life in the world. It can never be the prayer of a man alone.

I had understood this when I wrote two prayers. 'Why did you tell me I must love' and 'Before You Lord'. The first was inspired by the experiences of young activists who were discovering the meaning of charity by being more giving and open to each other; the second was perhaps misunderstood in its simplicity, but it dealt with the very necessary synthesis of the Christian's approach to God and to men: You will love the Lord your God with all your heart, all your body and all your soul, and you will love your neighbour as yourself.

353

Only Jesus Christ has a claim to 'human perfection'. Having voluntarily taken on bonds of solidarity with all his brothers and having transformed them into bonds of love, he became humanity. He embraced humanity, formed an alliance with it, and with it became 'one flesh'. Because Christ is perfection, every human being has become, through him, a part of him.

Because Jesus Christ is GOD, all parts of him, down to the tiniest, constitute the presence of God: 'You did it to ME' (Matthew 25:40).

354

Brazil of a thousand faces, who can come to you and not fall in love with you? I, like many others, wasn't able to resist you. I came as a lover, and as a lover I suffer in seeing you suffer.

BELOVED BRAZIL
Beloved Brazil, I stepped on your immense and generous
soil,
    your virgin earth, stripped of her clothing,
    your flesh red with the blood of your wounds,
    flesh offered in union, to whom? to what?
stolen earth snatched from the peons' arms, these ragged
couples
    with a heart of gold
    who sleep on you by night,
    and water you with their sweat and suffering by day,
raped earth, young girls submissive in the hands of pimps
    who will put you to work for their god
    Money.

Beloved Brazil, I visited your cities —
Brasilia, the city of the future,
Buildings jutting out unexpectedly, shocking the senses,
Tortured cities, disfigured lepers of poverty and hardship,
    concentration camps for the poor,
    where freedom has died,
Monstrous cities where the blue water of swimming pools
    and the red mud of the *favellas* coexist in an unholy
alliance.

Beloved Brazil, I caressed the faces of your young girls
with one look —
Hard, shining, ebony faces,
Marble tombstones covering buried, eternal memories
of whips and seared flesh,
Ivory skins, the milky whiteness of Europe that nourished
you,
Copper skins that no tanning aids, no beach in the world
can reproduce.

Beloved Brazil
I saw girls of your flesh being chased by your adopted
sons.
I heard the gnawing sound in your belly, the cries of your
oppressed,
And from the lips of your chained heroes, the cry of
freedom.
I watched your numberless believers rise, cherished of God,
filling your Church, covered by the Holy Spirit.

Beloved Brazil
Light and darkness,
Laughter and moaning,
Fire and blood,
Life and death,
Your tree grows in terrible majesty,
Twisted branches,
Broken branches,
    heavy with fruit.
Your tree, your enormous tree grows . . .
But why does it need so much blood,
    so much blood to grow?

355

Justice precedes love (how many Christians have forgotten
that!), but love doesn't necessarily follow justice. In other
words, it's impossible to love without being just, but you can
be just without loving, for while love presupposes justice,
it infinitely surpasses it.

356

Love and justice are not of the same order.

Does justice turn the other cheek? Is it justice to forgive — that is, to continue giving, when you have done me wrong? Is it justice to cancel your debt to me? Is it justice to let you out of prison when you deserve punishment?

It's not justice, it's love.

Loving means believing in others, in a faith that is full of hope, belief, support (see St Paul, Corinthians I:13 and following). As Christians, we must fight for justice, but we must also fight for love.

357

Love creates disorder in the existing order of things. Love can destabilise whole societies: unjust ones of course, but also just societies. This is why we are suspicious of the Gospel. The Gospel is too revolutionary.

358

Struggle is an integral part of man. He grows in and by struggle.

A baby struggles to physically separate from its mother.

A child struggles to be special in his parents' eyes.

An adolescent and a teenager struggle to become independent, then freely rejoin the family and society.

Couples struggle to retain their individuality within their marriage.

Groups struggle collectively to defend human rights and develop their identity.

Society struggles to obtain or defend its right to wealth, power and knowledge.

Without these struggles man cannot grow to become what he is — creator of himself and, with others, creator of humanity. At the heart of these struggles he unites with God who works constantly to 'make man' and humanity: Let us make man in our image.

In this context, struggle is 'christian'; it is the absence of struggle that is 'unchristian'.

359

Some people say (and think) that the class struggle is 'unchristian', while proclaiming that struggling in matters of business, such as absorbing, crushing, eliminating the competition, is just. What's more, having crushed their victims, they will award themselves all manner of honours and prizes in the name of competence, hard work and so on. They confuse their 'success' with virtue.

360

Individually or collectively, man has no rights which don't demand something in return. One man's rights necessarily involve the duties of another.

Pushing man to defend his rights without teaching him his duties is literally 'dismantling' him, throwing society off balance and finally blowing it all up in little pieces.

Demanding that man fulfil his duties without allowing him to defend his rights is to gag him, exploit him and finally create a society that will crush him.

361

Some people will tell you to first do your duty, then claim your rights. Others will counsel you to do the opposite. Both sides make bad shepherds. If you want to be a real person and build a just world, you must defend your rights and do your duty at the same time. But if your brothers are deprived of their essential rights, your first duty is to fight for them.

362

He's discouraged. Yesterday he said, 'We're fighting for nothing!'

That's not true. There are people everywhere fighting for one cause or another, a world of justice and peace, who are constantly brought to the brink of despair by the apparent unimportance or futility of their efforts. If, however, they can believe that their struggle, whatever the results, is an act of love, then they will win. True, authentic love always bears fruit. What's more, a Christian knows that God himself is committed to this. All love comes from God, said St John.

363

I meet many young adults (and some not so young) who have been 'used' by organisations to help keep some movement alive. Sooner or later they realised that they were just pawns in the hands of people who were out to win some game or other (even a legitimate one), that they were sucked in by their belief that they 'didn't exist just for themselves' and that taking care only of their own interests was a weakness. But having realised that they were being manipulated, they rebelled, they 'escaped'. And now they drag their unanswered questions around, ill at ease, in certain ways under-developed, in others over-developed, confused, violently rejecting the movement that used them, and the people who manipulated them. And some of them have quit, for ever. They have been accused of being uncharitable and told that if they were used, it was their own fault. But they're not guilty. The guilt lies with their teachers who didn't, in their teaching, respect certain indispensable and basic elements, and who decided for them rather than let them make their own decisions.

364

I seem to have dampened the enthusiasm of a family man I know. He told me that at home they'd been discussing the Third World and the campaign against hunger. His children broke open their piggy-banks and donated all their money.

And you, I said, did you break open your account?

We encourage children to be generous when we, ourselves, are far from showing that same kind of generosity. It is neither right nor healthy.

365

Man's commitment to his brothers is necessary to his own growth and development. But there are stages which must be respected.

To make adolescent demands of a child, or to make adult demands of an adolescent is to force them to a superficial maturation which can only end in sterility. We must all grow at our own pace.

366

Once in a while I'm violent, and when I am, I know it's because I'm weak. Isn't true strength the ability to control and channel one's violence into something constructive? I'm persuaded that strength is a sort of 'violence of love'. And I think that the violence of love is very close to what people call non-violence.

367

Kill to prevent more killings . . . yes; but kill him because he killed . . . never!

368

Only love enables humanity to grow, because love engenders life, and it is the only form of energy that lasts forever.

369

Who would dare tell working-class Christians and activists who are risking their lives struggling with their brothers for a decent standard of living, better working conditions, equal distribution of responsibility . . . who would dare tell them, and ask them to express it in their daily lives, that man's true happiness is infinitely beyond them and their very worthwhile goals? Who would dare run the risk of the violent arguments and fighting that would ensue? Who would dare expose himself to the attacks and condemnations and accusations of betrayal and desertion that would invitably follow? Who, if not Christians themselves? Because, if they don't who will?

370

At a meeting this afternoon (of the religious council general in Rome, where I was representing the French episcopal committee for Latin America), I was seated next to Father Arrupe. I had seen him before, listened to him and admired him, but never spoken with him. I was impressed by his ability to go to the heart of things, his large vision, his quiet strength, perhaps even his eagle-like profile. We exchanged a few words on the side, a bit like students in a boring class. I saw him as an eagle flying high above me, unattainable, but I discovered that he was also a lamb.

I'm happy this evening; also perhaps a little proud, and certainly enriched. You feel somewhat elevated when you've been in the company of great people. Like anyone else I need the company of these people, I admire them, but I'm overwhelmed when I find a human being behind the greatness.

Thank you Father Arrupe, thank you for being the Jesuits' general and their guiding light, and at the same time staying on our level, my level, accessible and . . . smiling.

371

Young people often get impatient and exasperated with all the advice that's given them. Why? Well, because before giving them advice, we should tell them why they need it in the first place.

What good are methods if you don't know what they're for.

372

Usually she's all smiles. Suddenly, today, storm clouds have broken over her life. And now here she is, crying, broken, like a tree hit by lightning. I want to dry her tears, I can't bear to see them; then I see that look in her eyes, a look of infinite sadness.

She's hurting inside. I know that it's her heart crying and I can't dry the tears of her heart.

Once again, I measure the distance separating beaten flesh and a bleeding heart. Only you, Jesus, from within, can dry the tears of the heart. I place her heart in your hands.

373

A month after his entry into a monastery, M. told us, 'I've discovered that the spiritual life is one long struggle. For me, for the Church, for the world, it's love's struggle more or less identical to all our different struggles wherever we might be.'

He's quite right. There is only one struggle, whether it involves an individual, a group, a social class, a people, or the mystic alone in his monastery. If the struggle is real and just, it is always one between selfishness and love. Everyone fights his corner, with his own weapons. But he needs other people. It is the same struggle undertaken by Jesus Christ. He is always present. Few recognise him, for he is unobtrusive, but there can be no victory without him.

Why do so many consider that, unless others fight with them, like them, on the same battlefield, they're sitting on the fence?

I'm bound to say to them, 'You need each other. You are indispensable where you are *if that is your rightful place.* Recognise each other; recognise your struggle. Thank each other and don't waste time in measuring the efficiency of your respective struggles. One struggle isn't more worthy or better fought than another. The only thing that counts is that the struggle be necessary and just, and that it be undertaken with love.'

374

R. is dead. I feel like weeping and screaming, and I'm not ashamed. I know that some consider tears to be a sign of weakness, and they could never understand that I can grieve for a son who isn't mine. They could never understand that I'm feeling like a father who's just lost his son. But Lord, am I worthless for not having fathered a child? Is the 'charisma' of celibacy nothing but an atrophied heart in reality? I am a man with a living, beating heart growing every day with love for sons I didn't ask for but whom you gave me. And now, one has been taken away from me and I can't bear it. No, I'm not ashamed to grieve; my grief is real, I'm profoundly wounded. Tomorrow I'll tell R.'s parents that I share their pain completely. But who can I turn to with my personal grief? Isn't this what they call loneliness?

TO DANNY, PIERRE, JEAN, STANNY, AND ALL THE
OTHERS, FOREMOST IN MY HEART

Children of my heart I saw you die and I couldn't accept it.
I weep, I cry, I can't express it,
For a father's grief is understood
But mine isn't — they say I don't have any children, I cannot
know.
All death is cruel — nothing is sadder than a blazing fire
suddenly being snuffed out.
I can understand a fire dying out when all the wood has
burned
But I can't understand a fire dying just after it's been lit,
the wood barely singed.
Children of my heart, I can never accept your disappear-
ance from this earth.
Your smooth young faces show no lines,
No wounds mark your bodies,
Your hair is untouched by a lover's caress,
You lips are unkissed by another's,
Your young bodies are unembraced,
You lie under marble, covered by earth.
Instead of giving us your sons, you gave us your deaths.
Children of my heart, you should be here, but you're not.
Your work was waiting
Men who needed you were waiting,
Soldiers of peace and justice were waiting for you on the
battlefield,
But you never came.
Your weapons are now rusting in the earth.
You were born on this earth but not into this life.
Your union with humanity will never be consumated.
Children of my heart, why did I love you so?
Were you not my sons and daughters I still would have
grieved,
But my heart wouldn't have bled so,
For your deaths, one by one, haven't frozen me —
I continue to suffer, my pain vivid as the day on which
you died.
Each one of you is always foremost in my heart.

Lord, you told me that if I followed you I would never be deprived of children. I believed you. I refused to have children, yet I was given them. You gave them to me, more than any loving woman could. But you never said, Lord, that in multiplying my sons you would be multiplying my suffering.

Those who came before us are alive, aren't they? In the twenty years that they lived, they lived a lifetime. You can't measure the value of a life by its length. I believe this, I think, but I need you to remind me of it this evening so that I can repeat it to you, in your own words, tomorrow.

There's only pain left now. What can I do? Give it to you? I'd like to. But please tell me that it's of some use, otherwise I'll never dare love again. It hurts too much.

375

(the day after R.'s funeral)
For two days now I've had one of Father Duval's songs on the brain. A song of wonderful simplicity which he used to sing for these young people, now gone from us before having even tasted life. The refrain which he played a touch violently on his guitar expressed my suppressed fury very well: 'And anger, the good Lord's anger, rises!'

I've never been tempted to hold God responsible for the death of young people. It would be making a mockery of my love for him. If I can put it this way, I think that God 'suffers' with us, more than us, for these young lives so brutally cut short, but that he is a 'prisoner of his own love', torn between his great desire to intervene and protect us from all mortal failures and wounds, and his will to love genuinely, that is, allowing us to be free and responsible for ourselves.

God is paternal, not paternalistic.

376

I have to believe, R., that your senseless death has some meaning, some use. It would be too dreadful to believe otherwise.

377

I've often said in conferences and on television that I wouldn't want a God who was some sort of puppeteer pulling the strings of humanity from the sky, allowing the good and blocking the evil. I've said that I wouldn't want a God who would offer us a perfect world on a silver platter, a ready-made, no-risk, guaranteed world populated by docile people brimming with love in a perfect society, where peace and justice are the norm. I said I would accept the price of freedom — pain and suffering — because freedom is indirect proof — the most beautiful and the most terrible — that we are loved.

But right now, cruelly wounded by the wounds of others, bearing their pain and mine, I am tempted, like a child accusing its parents, to doubt and yell with those who are shouting: Father, why didn't you intervene?

How easy it is to be brave when tragedy hits others! How easy to shrug off someone else's suffering. As long as it isn't happening to you, everything is fine.

378

The most searing thing about death is that it creates a physical absence. But physical absence doesn't mean *absence of presence*. I understood that a long time ago, after the war, when before me in my office a husband and wife were tearing each other apart. They overflowed with the bitterness and despair of couples who have loved each other but have grown apart. Suddenly the wife grasped her husband's arm and cried painfully: 'Remember how close, how united we were two years ago when you were a prisoner in Poland.' It is so true that genuine love can withstand distance. Julos Beaucarne (a French singer whose wife was murdered in the late 1970s) has some magnificent words: 'Death is just a different kind of presence.'

379

The bottom of your heart should be smooth, smooth enough for nothing to stick there. Then you can offer your brothers part of your riches. (Think of your heart as a skillet – if food sticks to a skillet, it burns and then you have problems 'reseasoning' it.)

If you keep things, or people, to yourself, your heart cannot function smoothly. Oh, it's difficult to love more than yourself!

380

You said: 'I don't give a d . . . about money.'

I replied: 'That's because you've got lots of it.'

A really poor person can't joke about money. It is the luxury – and the trap – of the very rich to think that they're indifferent to money.

381

There is no such thing as absence of God. If you think there is, it's because you're confused.

382

I've been worried for some time now about M. (a priest). There's something troubling him, but he won't say anything. His lips are sealed. He's completely locked up and unreachable. It's not that he isn't sensitive – he is – but his feelings are buried so deep in him as to be invisible. I feel for him.

I have great difficulty understanding a priest who doesn't know how to cry.

383

Humanity shouldn't be just a collection of individuals, but also a communion of people – the community. The way from one to the other is through freedom and love.

384

I get bored when I stop *trying* to give of myself. So why not give all the more? Everyone would benefit.

385

There are those who abandon power because they're afraid to use it.

There are others who let themselves be led for fear of being judged, or though lassitude.

There are those who willingly share power.

Make no mistake about it — only the latter can build a just world.

386

The Gospel is subversive no matter how you look at it, because it is the key to genuine and definitive liberation.

387

What motivates you? If you can truthfully reply: 'Jesus Christ', then continue, you're on the right path. But do you sometimes get carried away and forget the goal? You work to 'defend your rights', your work, your business, your parish and so on. Be careful — if you set yourself up in business for yourself, the Lord will let you work alone.

388

I don't feel I've loved enough, and it makes me sad. But I know that if I think too much about myself, I'll only get discouraged at my mediocrity. Better to think of God and his love; only that can nourish me with hope.

389

Man has the right to give life, one way or another, but he does not have the right to take it back, even if he 'didn't mean to give it' in the first place. The life he has engendered no longer belongs to him; it belongs to the person it was transmitted to. And if the latter cannot defend it (especially if he hasn't been born yet), then he must defend it for him. He is responsible for it.

There's little else one can say about the tragedy of

abortion. Certainly one must be infinitely understanding because this tragedy is sometimes provoked by great distress. But, like it or not, snatching a seed that has already taken root out of the earth, or a seed that's already become a tiny plant growing in the sun, is *stopping* life and condemning its flower to death.

390

What is true for abortion holds true for all attacks on life. Some abortions are called 'condemnation to death', some 'work-related accidents'; then there are abortions which result from bad housing, dangerous working conditions, world hunger, underdevelopment. . . . Every year many millions of lives are 'aborted' before their time. In the end we shall have to account to God for all these unjustly interrupted lives.

Why are some people shocked at aborted babies and not at these deaths? Because they weren't planned, because they weren't directly provoked? Because we are responsible *together*? Certainly, circumstances differ widely and no one can judge another's responsibility, but let's be quite honest about this, when it comes to defending life we cannot separate some from others, on merit or whatever. To be true and credible, we must defend *all* life, and defend it with equal fervour.

391

In a general fashion I think men are more selfish than women. A woman is more naturally inclined to give and receive, and I don't see why women these days get annoyed when they're told this.

Only a woman knows how to really love; a man needs a woman to teach him. She can bring him out of himself and show him a whole new world he never knew existed. Thanks to her, he can discover new emotions and new riches, even if they do make him more vulnerable.

Woman is sent to man to teach him how to love. I think that celibacy, even dedicated celibacy, is easier for a woman than a man. For a celibate, who could ever replace a woman, that powerful magnet which draws him out of himself, not just now, today, but tomorrow and forever? Christ and mankind? Yes, but a 'relationship' with Christ and the 'will' to serve mankind are not enough — you must be 'in love' with Christ and 'passionate' about mankind. Without passion, celibacy cannot be positive, that is, generate love and create life.

392

Once again I find myself confronted by death, and I need to think about it. There have been times when death has brushed my sleeve. I'm not talking about the obituary columns in the daily papers, or the dead I am asked to bury at church (as if the church was made for burials!), because these dead, whatever their circumstances, are unknown to me. Their deaths haven't hit me personally. I'm talking, rather, about 'my' deaths — mine or the death of those I hold dear, who have become part of me (for that is what loving does) and who take a little piece of me away with them. Then I think of the absurd and seemingly futile deaths that are imposed on me almost defiantly, a monstrous insult to life.

The first death I witnessed was that of my father. I still remember it. I was twelve years old. My mother had gone out in the middle of the night to find a doctor (who was proving to be elusive just when he was needed); my sister was in boarding school, and I was there alone with my dying father. We made a tragic twosome. I was terrified. I held his face in my trembling hands. He was unable to speak, his eyes were blank and he was perspiring terribly. I mopped his face but the perspiration kept flowing. And so did my fear. I was obsessed with one thought; what if he dies before Mum gets back? I would be holding a dead person, my first death, and this first death would be my Dad (he died the following day in hospital). (Note: Since writing the above, I have lost my mother. She was nearly 91. It wasn't her death itself that hurt me, it was the slow creeping knowledge that sooner or later death would come and take a life we had so loved; a fire that peters out, bit by bit, is so infinitely sad.)

My second meeting with death was my own peaceful,

almost joyous brush with death. I was sixteen. I was returning home from a JOC congress in Paris in a happy, delirious mood. I'd just seen the path I'd been searching for sprawled before me, clear, brightly lit. I'd found the way, the one the LIVING Jesus Christ walked on.

The next day, in the afternoon, I was rushed to hospital. Twenty-four hours of worry and anguish (which I didn't know about) and on the second night, overhearing my aunt talking with the night nurse. 'How old is he?' — 'Sixteen.' — 'What do the doctors say?' — 'They think he won't last more than two or three hours at most.' — 'I can't bear it, he's so young.'

I heard it all. You have to be careful what you say in front of dying people. But I had to be sure. So I asked my mother, 'What did the night nurse say?' My mother muttered some lie or other. I insisted. She got stubborn. Then I stopped her and said, 'Don't worry yourself, give me a kiss!' She couldn't though, my condition didn't permit kissing. She held my hand tight (I can still feel the pressure). I knew she was crying, but I couldn't see her because I was blind. I hurt because she hurt.

What followed was very simple. I offered my life to the Lord, for the JOC, for my friends. It seemed to me the thing to do since I was a 'militant'. I was quite calm. I wasn't suffering. But death wouldn't come, so to pass the time, I started imagining all the wreaths that would be sent to my funeral; I tried to imagine the looks on the pall bearers' faces, the degree of sincerity in their words and tears. I remember being quite hard on them!

The next morning I was surprised to find myself still among the living. I waited and waited. Well, I'm still waiting. But that's another story.

Today, would I 'experience' my impending death in the same way? I don't think so; it's difficult to say. At sixteen, I didn't know much about life. I had no particular attachment to it so it wasn't difficult to give it up. I think that now, though, despite my mad trust in my love for the Father, it would hurt me to offer him a mediocre life. This is not humility — I'm just being realistic, accepting the clear and cruel gap between what we have 'dreamed', what we have understood and what we have lived.

But no matter! It's nothing to do with imagining one's death. One must live now, today, that's all.

My third encounter with death was through the senseless, brutal, futile, odious massacre and bloodshed of war.

After the landings, I was in Paris, and before the general paralysis set in, I hopped aboard one of those rare trains leaving out of the Gare Saint-Lazare for Le Havre. As a seminarian, I was supposed to meet a group of children whom we were sheltering outside the city. I heard later that we numbered fifty-six on the ghost train moving through the night with all its lights switched off, in total darkness so as not to attract the enemy fire and all those guns going off out there. We were two in my compartment. My companion was a young man with whom I talked a little. Then he fell asleep, and after a while so did I. An almighty jolt woke me up. I found myself on the floor, covered in shattered glass — I wasn't hurt, not even a scratch. I tried to move, feeling my way around. All the windows and doors of the train were gone. Right before me, on the ballast, I saw my companion lying on his back, dead. There was a fire burning — I remember the red flames leaping up in the dark. The train had been hit by a string of incendiary bombs. The quiet countryside was now pierced with the cries of the wounded and the dying, and the shouting of some German soldiers running away in the distance. Nearby a young boy, no more than fifteen, his leg smashed, trembled and cried. I tried to calm him: 'Don't be afraid, it's all over.' It wasn't true. The aeroplanes kept coming back, flying very low and firing again and again. Finally, their mission accomplished, they left. The train was one long blazing fire. I gave the boy . . . an aspirin: 'Take this, it's very strong medicine!' I told him. I tied my scarf around his leg and stretched him out on a wooden plank someone (there must have been only four or five of us left) had unearthed. His crushed leg hung there useless. I would place it back on the plank and it would slip off making the boy scream with pain. So I took out my knife and cut it off. A little further the engine driver whimpered pitifully, 'I'm thirsty.' A shell had ripped his belly apart. I didn't have any water. Some people had already arrived on the scene and were taking the wounded away in makeshift ambulances.

Later on I went to see the engine driver in hospital. He was already dead. But the boy had survived. The nurse told me I'd saved his life by amputating his leg.

I went back to the carnage with three other men to see what could be done about cleaning it all up. They had brought some burlap sacks for the corpses and all the human bits and pieces strewn around. It was so ghastly that they couldn't face it. But it had to be done, so I asked them to hold the sacks open and began collecting the pieces.

Most of these pieces were caught on the barbed wire around a nearby field. It was a horrifying spectacle of human butchery — the worst was a head sliced off from its body, lying in the grass. For an instant I was chilled. Then, under the horrified gaze of my companions, I picked it up by the hair, looked at it, then put it in the sack. The man — it was a man's head — had his eyes open, staring, frozen, stupified; open but unseeing.

It was very heavy. My arm couldn't take it, so I put it in the sack.

The 'body bags' were then taken to the nearest town hall. I stopped there for a while to collect myself, before going on to the hospital to visit the wounded. A young man was looking in the sacks, staring, haggard and babbling, 'It's my brother-in-law, my little brother-in-law . . . he got married the day before yesterday . . .' he repeated pitifully. I put my hand on his shoulder. He didn't move, but like a needle stuck in a record, he kept repeating, 'my little brother-in-law, my little brother-in-law. . . .'

I said nothing. There was nothing I could say.

I realised then, that apart from talking to the young man whose leg was amputated, I had scarcely spoken a word since the nightmare began. I had remained calm, impassive, oblivious to fear, almost cold — the only feeling I had was one of total revulsion that totally blocked any normal feelings.

Yes, it was absurd, odious and incredibly futile — enough to make one scream. Futile, senseless destruction of human lives and all for NOTHING.

There. Tonight, the death of others had sent me back to this awful memory and I've relived it by writing it down. I ask myself why. Do I need to exorcise a vague feeling of anguish that's hovering around my soul? I don't think so. Naturally, like anyone else, with every year that passes, I feel I've less time left. As it happens I love life and I feel that I'm not wasting mine (so I'm told). But I also feel that death musn't be wasted either; in fact, less so than life. You couldn't do it unless you were well prepared.

Faced with death, my first reaction was one of *fear*. Then, having consciously accepted and offered it up, I experienced an incredible feeling of peace. Finally, I came across this dreadful, meaningless death, of men slaughtering each other when all they really wanted was to live.

It's obvious enough that I desperately wish for an 'offered' death — Oh Lord, if only I could give you in the night what I couldn't give my brothers during the day.

393

(on a flight, returning from Canada)

I want to be faithful. But I can't always manage it. I admit I was prey to 'human' temptation — by the invitation to lecture in Montreal's magnificent Olympic stadium before an audience of 40,000 to 70,000 people (at least, according to the newspapers). My lecture was scheduled towards the end of the North American Charismatic Congress. Who could resist such an audience? I didn't know it at the time, but the television station covering the congress decided to show the closing addresses live, so in fact I was addressing several million people. What a responsibility. I didn't give it too much thought, probably to keep myself humble.

Come to think of it, why did I agree to come in the first place? Well, initially because the organisers insisted with numerous telephone calls demanding an immediate, and positive, answer. Then my friend said, 'Go on!' And finally I had the temerity to think that I had something to say to all these people, something unusual and unexpected and which I thought I could vigorously proclaim!

I chose the Gospel of St Matthew on the Last Judgement (Ch. 24, 31, 46), a text that I've always been very attached to and even obsessed with. I know what I'm talking about because this commitment of Christ — all the way to identifying himself with the poorest of the poor — constantly judges and condemns me. The risen Christ is there in our lives. We brush against him daily. We meet him in suffering and death. We don't often recognise him and we pass him by as we look up above, searching the sky for him.

While I spoke at the stadium, a plane circled above displaying a banner that read 'We bear witness to the Resurrected Christ'. It seemed to be a very telling symbol of the 'disincarnation' of Christ.

Hallelujahs were bursting deliriously around me like fireworks and I was obliged to throw some water on them. I needed silence while I spoke – and I got it. The crowd listened, motionless. For one second I saw myself projected onto a giant electronic screen at one end of the stadium. Then I looked at the vibrating mass of humanity before me, and once again I took off, like a boxer in the ring determined to win the fight. When I finished speaking, the delirium started up again. The entire stadium trembled and groaned, ending in a violent crescendo of cries, gestures, chanting . . . miracles? Was it the Holy Spirit? Perhaps I lack the proper amount of faith, but I don't find this sort of thing convincing. Or, at least, I *believe*, the way I believe that he is present in every sincere Christian, in every church community, in every person of good will working alone or with others for the common good. No more, no less.

I thought hard as I looked at this crowd. No bishop or movement could have assembled this many people, certainly not in the last few dozen years. My Canadian friends said that at one time, in the 'old days', religious gatherings, parades, certain feast days and so on used to bring the crowds out and unite all kinds of people. I wondered if we hadn't over-intellectualised our Christianity and other religions. Haven't we forgotten that Christians are human after all? We can't very well be surprised if they turn around and vent their frustration and let it all pour out whenever they get a chance, in ways and words that often make us uneasy?

After all, I believe strongly enough in the Holy Spirit to know without a doubt that he will certainly guide many in this crowd of starving people towards Jesus Christ who waits . . . around the corner.

394

Convincing man that happiness lies in consumerism is making him dependent, and indeed enslaving him, to material goods.

395

I don't know if it was because I was tired or over-anxious, but I have no worthwhile memories of an important meeting I attended at the United Nations with Abbé Pierre. I can, however, write about the meeting itself, for the record.

All I can say, to begin with, is that I was momumentally bored, the way you can get bored watching a very bad movie. And while you can walk out of a cinema, I couldn't walk out of this session.

I hadn't brought anything to read, more's the pity. I had nothing to scribble on. I was stuck. All i could do was wait until the session was over. Not even the fact that I was in a room full of international VIPs moved me. These were the people who made decisions and history? They were just like anyone else — mortals, with a nose and eyes and mouth and ears. And to those I met in the corridors I could very easily have said, 'Sit down, gentlemen, let's discuss your problems.'

And what of this dissipated assembly, chatting to their neighbours, writing (I wonder what), yawning, dozing, while someone on the podium talks interminably? This is the United Nations? It's more like a huge human comedy. And I'm on the world's stage! Watching today's show! It seems, though, that little happens, if anything (I'm told the real action takes place before the show, during rehearsals). I gave up listening to the speeches. Instead, I tried to pray, I day-dreamed.

This morning, on my way into the UN building, I noticed a luxurious building nearby which turned out to be a 'canine clinic'. It's a fine state of affairs when animals are better treated and cared for than humans, at least in certain parts of the world.

For their part, men continue to suffer and die by the millions. Well, let them be patient! Their representatives are busy making speeches.

396

Determinism controls much of our lives today. Freedom is not freeing yourself from determinism, but being free in spite of it.

397

These days I often mix with the 'outside world' (to use religious jargon), or the upper middle class, as some would call it. I appreciate their upbringing and culture and refinement. I find their homes very comfortable and their wines superior — no mere table wine plonk! Since I visit them in a 'good cause', that of my ministry, since they're good Christians who seek to live according to the Gospel, our relationship goes well beyond after-dinner pleasantries. We're friends, I like them, I love their children. In short, I feel comfortable with them. But there are times when I feel somewhat revolted — not by them, but by the monstrous injustice that, under the guise of normality, has made them what they are today, living the good life. At best, they owe it to their parents' or grandparents' hard work. They owe it to their upbringing. That's all very well, but there are other parents and grandparents who have worked just as hard, perhaps harder, and have given their children just as good an upbringing, but have never attained the same recognition — level, or class, if I can put it that way. It's unjust and the upper classes know it. They say, 'We know we're privileged, but . . . it's not our fault!' It's certainly not a sin to be rich (with a few exceptions), but it is an enormous responsibility.

What can they do about it? What can I advise them to do? Give up their comfortable lifestyle, their background, careers, culture, winter sports and summer holidays? You'd have to be crazy! Of course, I ask them to work towards the common good; I push them to combat injustice by using their influence; but I pity them. It's so much easier to fight for what you don't have, than to fight to have part of what you do have taken away from you. Oh it's not easy being rich!

As I look at their children, I think, 'Parents, if you are Christians and you love your children, don't turn them into "rich" adults!!'

398

Death is absurd and meaningless if it is not 'humanised'. Animals are born, they live and die without knowing it, therefore without knowing why and for whom they were born.

Life is imposed on man just as it is on animals, but with a difference. Man can look for meaning to his life and make his own decisions. In accepting life and committing himself consciously and freely in the act of his own creation as well as the world's, he becomes human, a man — but not before he accepts his death in the same spirit. Death is the one supreme occasion on which he can testify that life was given him for the sole purpose of being passed on and perpetuated.

399

(during a study session)

Again I get the dreadful impression that God's Word is being massacred. I really resent people who insist on dissecting God in their laboratories, performing autopsies and presenting us with the bits and pieces of a cadaver. St Paul tells us that the Word *lives*; I say that these so-called specialists *kill* it.

When I was only fifteen and (thanks to a friend and the JOC) had just met the living Christ in the streets (through the gift of others, fuelled by the movement's activities), I discovered the Gospel and the Epistles. It was a great, dazzling moment in my life. I could quote today words that touched me so deeply that they are forever embedded in my mind as a source at which I quench my thirst now and then.

My friend Jean and I must certainly have misinterpreted certain words and passages, when together, we would read them by the light of a street lamp or on the beach.

I don't doubt that, later on, in groups, we made mistakes when we pronounced our own commentaries on whatever passage we happened to be reading, occasionally being corrected by the chaplain in charge of us. And I'm sure I made mistakes at the seminary for late vocations during morning meditation — throughout the whole first term, I was glued to the passage on the Samaritan woman.

Mistakes or not, I wish everyone could have the same experience. I myself drank avidly from that source. I opened my soul wide to receive the seed, even though brambles and thorns grew up. I know that without the Word I wouldn't be here; everything I learned subsequently nourished my spirit perhaps, but rarely my heart. In any case, I'm sure that all the studying in the world could not have changed me as radically, and thrown me into the adventure that shook my whole life.

400

We all worry about what others think of us. A person judges himself by what others think of him; if their opinion isn't too good, he worries, sometimes over-reacts, and becomes a slave to that opinion (or 'quoted value'!).

So you think you're more or less immune to what others think of you? Do you really think you don't care what they think? Isn't it because you believe yourself to be liked?

The only opinion that should concern you is the opinion God holds of you. I'm not talking about a god who talks directly to you, or one you have fashioned in your imagination, but a God who expresses himself through the Church and your community. You may then see your 'quoted value' drop, for God's opinion is rarely the same as man's.

401

Life and love at the heart of this life cannot die. They transform each other.

Dying is just the beginning of a new form of life.

402

Death is awesome — it comes like a wrenching in the night. It demands total abandon and blind faith in life. Death is therefore the supreme test, the supreme suffering. This suffering can be transformed through Jesus Christ, because he based the Redemption on it.

403

Life after death is unimaginable. Think of a baby in its mother's womb — if it could think, it could never imagine what life out of the womb would be like. A baby has to have blind faith in its mother who carries it within her and prepares to bring it into another world.

Thus a dying man must have faith in the forces of nature which push him towards a place where 'the Father waits on the threshhold of his House,' to paraphrase a well-put line of a funeral hymn.

404

When we mourn the death of our loved ones, we should make sure that our tears aren't wasted. Each tear shed can make life grow if we offer it up, through and with Jesus Christ.

405

Speak Lord; your servant is listening . . .

If only I had faith! If only I loved enough to come before you — small, humble and loving, to read the love letter you sent to your Church and all mankind through your evangelists. Too often that letter remains untouched on my bedside table, even though I know you'd like me to read it with you. And I know that you could explain its meaning to me.

A person reading a love letter doesn't study and analyse it as if it were a literary text or a political manifesto or a legal document, or some kind of a laboratory specimen. It's not that he's not intelligent or literate, just that he's reading it with the eyes of love, unconcerned with grammar or style, his heart leaping towards his love through the words on paper. A love letter, after all, is just a means of uniting two lovers.

Lord, I know that you sent your letter to each and every one of us. You want to reveal yourself to me, you want to trust me. Speak Lord, your friend is listening. I would like to be able to write to you too and tell you that 'your lover is listening.'

406

Dying doesn't mean the end of life but the end of love (that's why moralists have qualified 'big sins' as 'mortal').

407

Our eternal 'vitality' will be measured by the intensity of our love for our fellow beings, over the span of our lifetime.

'Heaven' is loving in Christ, to the rhythm of the Trinity.

408

Pay attention to *the day in hand.* You can never have it back once it's passed. There is not one single day that we can ever relive. If you could be happy to live today with no hankering after yesterday (it's out of your reach now), with no yearning for tomorrow (you don't even know if it will come), you would fill your present with all your heart and energy and life. And you would truly live!

409

I spoke of the Gospel, or on the Gospel, to those who asked me for explanations. I then noticed that too often I used the Scriptures to illustrate and validate my own thinking. Now what I strive for is to bring two beings together: Christ and the person, or persons, searching for him. I'm the intermediary. I introduce them, that's all. To be able to listen to and talk with someone, you need to know who he is, and how his mind works.

I discovered that all I had to do was clarify a few essential points, withdraw discreetly, and let the newly introduced people discover each other on their own.

I have never regretted this. On the contrary, I have been very gratified when someone I have 'introduced' to the Lord has confided in me what Christ has told him.

410

Suffering is an affliction, a waste. It is a sign that man is not yet in control of the universe, and that humanity is not yet a community triumphant in love.

To those who so often come to me with their suffering, I must not, under the pretext of faith, talk to them of 'offering it up'; I must first help them hear the call to battle that rings at the core of every suffering. Then I can invite them to join Jesus Christ, and to bear and offer *with* him.

411

It is not Jesus Christ's suffering that saved the world — it is the *love* with which he bore and offered his suffering. Wood cannot burn without a fire to consume it.

Only love engenders life.

412

Sin is always loving badly, or not loving at all.

Redemption is Jesus Christ restoring to the world the full weight of love — of which man robbed it through his sin.

413

I took the announcement of Father Riobé's death very badly. I was shocked to hear high praise coming from people who had denigrated him when he was alive. But he's dead now; I don't suppose he'll trouble them any more. I was shocked because I loved him.

Dear Father Riobé, I loved your square appearance, your large, strong, dry handshake (I always shudder when I'm offered a limp, wet hand). I loved your bursting, hearty, even abrupt manner. No unctious, oily, overblown words ever came from you, but only precision and clarity. I loved discussing things with you and the way your mind worked; I admired your ability to admit that you were wrong, when you were wrong. I loved your uncanny intuition, those shooting stars of insight, arrested in flight and put down on pieces of paper; and yet you also thought things out carefully, consulted friends and experts alike, no matter what one might think (I know, I was there).

I loved to watch you in those boring meetings we would get stuck in — you seemed even more bored than me. We'd secretly smile at each other, but sooner or later, your face would tense up. You never uttered a word while others talked and discussed and verbalised. Uneasy at your silence, someone would eventually ask you, 'And you, Father Riobé, what do you think?' 'Nothing,' you'd mumble. And all the while the tension would continue rising; I could feel it and I would wait for the eruption. It came soon enough. In a few short, clear, rich phrases, you said exactly what needed to be said — trenchant and true. And everyone knew it, except for a handful who would grumble that 'Father Riobé had acted up again'.

On leaving you'd say to me, 'I should have kept my mouth shut!' And I would reply, 'No, no, someone had to say it — but, perhaps you could have softened the delivery a little . . .?'

We would then go and have a jar in a bistro where you were happy to chat with the regulars (who didn't know who you were). I loved you all the more for the courage of your ways, attitudes, convictions, declarations — for saying out loud what others thought (I know, people have told me). But these same people didn't lift a finger to defend you when you spoke up on unpopular issues and were opposed by the guardians of the status quo, or, worse, when they smiled condescendingly at you. Many people distrust 'prophets', especially when they're bishops. They prefer their prophets to be very wise, and when one of them throws a cat among the pigeons, well, it inconveniences them.

Dear Father Riobé, I also loved you because you were the only person who, on more than one occasion, suggested we pray together when the going was rough. You would take me to your little makeshift chapel, and there we would sit in deep silence for a few moments. I would watch you while I prayed. You had simply said, 'Come, let's pray,' in much the same way you would say, after hours of hard work, 'Come, let's go and have a shot of whisky . . . we've earned it.' I will always cherish those moments with you.

Father Riobé, I was never familiar enough with you to call you by your Christian name, Guy. When I first met you a long time ago in Paris, it wasn't done; and when you were named a bishop, it was definitely not the thing to do. I was also too timid, and afraid of an adverse reaction on your part. I can hear you say, 'Idiot!' You'd have probably been

224

quite pleased for me to address you by your first name, because you needed that sort of familiarity at times. But you knew I felt this way, didn't you? You know it even more today. Now that you're dead, some people have become your friends, but I, I loved you when you were alive.

414

There would be no struggle if the world were perfect, and men were perfect. But this isn't the case.

Struggle, then, is an integral part of man, his growth and the growth of the world. Neither can grow without struggle.

415

Christians often equate charity with non-violence — an idea that's totally wrong. Struggling against others is not proof of an absence of love, quite the contrary. Man, whether individually or collectively, that is to say, in groups, movements or social classes, must be capable of saying to others, 'If you love me authentically, some day or other you will have to fight against me if I stop you from fulfilling yourself, and I want to love you so that I am capable of struggling against you when you will not permit me to be myself. 'In this sense he who struggles rejoins to make man ('Let us make man in our image') free and responsible, and the world, just.

416

All struggles for liberation must be 'purified'. If they are motivated by hatred, envy, revenge, they may break the chains of bondage, but they'll never destroy them. Broken chains can be put together again, and used to enslave just as before. So the struggle for liberation will have to continue as long as men continue to enslave their fellow men.

Only struggle motivated by love can once and for all smash the chains of bondage and break the vicious circle of violence.

417

All causes are not necessarily just, and when they're not, we have no right to support them even in the name of solidarity — whether with our brothers, within a group or movement or organisation.

There are some causes a Christian could never espouse, and there are tactics he could never use. This is why it's so difficult for him to commit himself.

418

Deep down, I'm not a joyful person, even if I do sometimes act the clown. But I believe that to live, one needs laughter, and I meet many people who have this need. They're often gloomy and, worse, take themselves too seriously. I don't think that I'm like that myself, though there are people who make me out to be a 'serious' person. And that's when I get an irresistible urge to joke around and make them laugh. I'd have liked to be a professional clown!

But all of this is superficial anyway, because deep down, I'm not like that. There are two reasons for this — the sometimes obsessive thought that so much of the world is suffering, and a tearing desire for a 'beyond' I cannot reach. I see it as a land to which I have no access. I set up camp on its frontiers, and the few times I venture into its neighbouring lands, far from pacifying me, only sharpen my desire.

419

Yesterday, once again, among a gathering of young people, fresh, wonderfully healthy, without hang-ups and bursting with life and joy, I found myself overcome by a sadness — the kind that can either seep into you or hit you abruptly — that settled deep within me. Yet there was only one thing to do, and that was to listen, watch, welcome and *be happy* for their joy. I was happy for them, but not for me. As usual, my mind was on the fact that so many people don't know, and will never know, this sort of happiness. Why should some be happy and others not?

When I open the door to my heart slightly to peep out,

I am inspired to open its windows wide. Then I see the suffering multitudes, near or far, bleeding and dying. And my little happinesses disappear. I've seen too much misery to forget.

I hear people say, 'If we thought of the world's suffering all the time, we could never live!' So, to live, we try not to think too much. I've tried it too, without much success; I've tried to rid myself of this heavy weight I drag around with me. My inability to be happy while others are miserable condemns me to be secretly, and all too often, unhappy. I can't help it. Am I abnormal? I think that I'm just logical. I say to myself, 'If you had lots of brothers and sisters, could you be happy and carefree while one of them slaved away, another was being tortured to death, and another was dying of hunger and thirst? If you take your relations with people seriously, especially if you're a Christian, and you can recite that Our Father in all sincerity with your brothers in church, you couldn't possibly be completely happy while others aren't.'

Trying to be a real person and a real Christian, that is to say, to commit yourself to supporting mankind where all members are your 'kin', necessarily involves suffering with them, for them, and fighting to lessen their suffering.

420

I sat on the ground, leaning against a tree, reading. I felt like dropping my book and just gazing at the scenery around me. But I made myself continue reading. I must finish this book, I told myself insistently. It wasn't easy, and in the end I gave in to the beauty of the countryside which cried out for my attention and admiration.

A simple, beautiful sight — neatly planted fruit trees, a forest beyond, silent and motionless. The only movement came from the setting sun, slowly dying on the horizon, flooding everything with its last rays dancing in the silence. I felt the trees were secretly alive, watching me, in either a mocking, disappointed or sad way . . . They probably pitied me because I had to move to live, while they could peacefully stand there year after year.

It was time to get up. I looked at the trees one last time — a faint breeze rustled in them, and it seemed the trees were waving goodbye.

Lord, I know you are in our lives, but you are also in nature. We so often forget that. But how are we to read the message in your open book? Have we systematically closed it?

In the city, not one inch of space remains untrodden. The modern world has covered the earth in a black shroud and nailed it firmly down. The renovators have come in and surrounded trees in concrete and steel. Before long, one will have to pay a fee to visit the earth!

Nature is poetry! But so is *life*. Man is earth. Torn from it, he loses his bearings and becomes a legless, footless 'brain', at the mercy of the spirit that sweeps him away from reality — like a balloon floating away to wherever the wind blows it.

Man must rediscover his ties with the earth.

421

My deepest joy comes from the happiness of others. I welcome it, when I am able, without a second thought — since it is not my personal happiness, it does not involve selfishness.

422

People in love often worry about being too happy. I can understand that. I feel the same way with my own little joys, like a child who wants something but doesn't know if it has the right to take it. Little joys I barely touch for fear of grabbing them, and clinging to them; little joys leaving traces of bitterness because they're not shared; little joys that make me feel guilty because I imagine I've stolen them from those who have none.

Yet I know, Lord, that happiness is not a sin. You yourself preached happiness. I should be able to take any I am offered — but only to give to you. Why should I only offer you thorns, while flowers fade and die on the roadside of my life? I do realise though, that just as we can be trapped by misery, so can we get carried away selfishly by our happiness, forgetting all else. We must be pure enough to welcome without clinging.

I have the right to be happy, *if it helps me serve others better.*

423

Lately I've often looked over some of my notes, read and reread them. I've decided to send them to a publisher, but I hesitate because I want to be sure first that they're interesting, and helpful enough, to be published.

There were many people in the lecture hall last night. They all listened to me intently. When I finished speaking, I walked down the aisle to the exit, and felt everyone's eyes on me. I had a strange impression that they were looking at me in an odd way, surprised, mesmerised. I suddenly felt uncomfortable — as if I'd undressed before them and was walking naked down this interminable aisle.

What should I do? Speak of myself? Refrain from speaking completely? Many of my friends urge me to speak; some say nothing — how do I interpret their silence?

I think, actually, that it's a false dilemma. The problem isn't one of whether to speak or not, but of being *true, real.* Why should priests ask others to talk of themselves, their experiences, their faith, without ever talking of their own? The main thing is not to perform a spiritual striptease to seduce weak souls.

424

I know that man's greatest problems arise out of a lack of love. I know this intellectually, and from experience. I see it. I touch it with my fingertips when, silently and attentively, I listen to someone's problems and unhappiness. Then I see the chasm in his life, and I am only too happy to be able to offer some love, combined with that of the Lord and transfigured by him, to fill that chasm.

There are times, however, that I feel I've used up too much of that love on myself; I've precious little left to give, and the other leaves, comfortless, the chasm still gaping and empty. My inability to love him and thereby help him to love, will make him suffer.

425

I can't for one moment believe that there isn't a world 'beyond', I don't mean a faraway place somewhere at the end of time, but a 'beyond' *within* all things, all people, all life.

I can't believe that there is nothing beyond the sea, the wind, the sky and the stars, beyond flowers and fruit. I can't believe that there is nothing beyond the world and history — this world, this history — and joy and suffering. I can't believe that there's nothing but wounded flesh or the touch of other flesh.

No, I can't believe that behind the suffering and death of untold millions who have fought for man, his freedom and dignity, there's nothing but condemned bodies hungry for bread.

No, I can't believe that behind the love of a husband and wife, or a mother, lies only copulation and territorial defence. And, especially, when I look at you, Man, and look deep into your eyes and see in there all your suffering and joy, I can't for one moment believe that at the end of your path, there is no exit, that you are in a dead-end.

And when, overcome by the mystery of man, I stop in my tracks and think, I can't believe that this interior beyond is just a blind force, a sort of faceless life. No, if it can be called anything, it must be called LOVE.

So, while continuously I collide with beings and things — with my fingertips, my eyes, my soul and my heart — a strong desire to meet the FACE of the beyond rises in me.

I love the sea, the wind, the sky and the stars. I love flowers and fruit. I love people and life. But to stroke the FACE, I must unclench my earthly fists which, in my small moments of grace, I feel I can open wide if I want to.

If I must close the eyes of my body to *see* the one who is *Love*, then I will . . .

But, Lord, is my faith strong enough? Do I believe enough? Will I not be afraid?

Have I, above all, made you sufficiently part of my life, have I borne witness enough, I who too often hide your light from others?

I still have much work to do. I must walk on, tied up in knots as I am, heavy and divided, with the taste of the earth and the sky mingling in my mouth. I must fight alongside man, for man. I must prod and worry him, get him out into the open and push him onto the road of the OTHER.

I must tell him that I am searching with him, at his side —
but that I know who I'm searching for, and I search *without seeing.*

O my God! *I know that you are there!*